A 365 Day Devotional of Reflections and Prayers
for Busy Moms

HAPPY HEALTHY & HOLY

Danielle Thienel

Author of The Cyclone Mom Method and The Peaceful
Mind Bible For Busy Moms

Introduction

In the whirlwind of motherhood, finding moments for spiritual connection can feel impossible. Yet these moments of divine connection are exactly what sustain us through busy days and challenging seasons. This devotional was born from my own desire, as a Catholic mom, to start each day grounded in faith while managing the practical demands of family life. Its purpose is to help lead you to being more of the Happy, Healthy, and Holy mom God created you to be.

Each daily reading combines Scripture, reflection, prayer, and a positive thought to carry with you. These devotions emerged from the topics discussed on episodes of The Peaceful Mind Podcast for Catholic Moms, as well as conversations with hundreds of moms through my coaching practice. They address the real struggles we face - from managing our time and emotions to building stronger relationships and deeper faith.

This isn't just a collection of inspirational thoughts. It's a practical tool for transformation, blending timeless Catholic wisdom with actionable strategies for peaceful living. Each day's message aims to help you:

- Center yourself in God's presence
- Shift perspective from overwhelm to peace
- Take small steps toward positive change
- Build confidence in your divine purpose
- Find joy in daily moments

Whether you read these pages in the quiet of early morning, during a quick afternoon break, or as you wind down at night, my prayer is that these words serve as gentle reminders of God's constant presence in your motherhood journey.

Let's walk together through these pages, finding renewed peace and purpose in our sacred calling as mothers, leading us to a happier, healthier, and holier life.

In Christ's Peace,

Danielle

PRAYER
Healing Father, help me to embrace the necessary pain of growth and change. Give me courage to feel deeply without becoming overwhelmed, knowing You are present in my pain. Thank You for using every experience, even the difficult ones, to shape me more into Your image. Grant me peace in knowing that this pain serves a purpose in my journey of healing. Amen.

POSITIVE THOUGHT OF THE DAY
My pain has purpose and leads to healing when I embrace it with God.

January 14th

Nurturing Growth Through Clean Parenting

SCRIPTURE
"Train the young in the way they should go; even when old, they will not swerve from it." - Proverbs 22:6

REFLECTION
Consider your approach to parenting today. Are your actions and reactions coming from a place of love and intention, or from fear and frustration? 'Clean parenting' means engaging with your children from a place of positive intent, guiding them through their difficulties with compassion rather than control. Today, choose to parent from a place that reflects the values you cherish and the love you hold for your children, fostering a home filled with understanding and grace.

PRAYER
Gentle Father, guide me in parenting with intention and love. Help me respond to my children from a place of wisdom rather than reaction. When frustration rises, remind me to pause and choose my responses carefully. Thank You for modeling perfect parental love. Help me reflect Your patient, nurturing spirit in my own parenting. Amen.

POSITIVE THOUGHT OF THE DAY
I parent with intention, choosing love over fear in each moment.

January 15th

Leading with Clarity and Love

SCRIPTURE
"Let love be sincere; hate what is evil, hold on to what is good." - Romans 12:9

January

January 1st

Embracing Peace in the Midst of Motherhood

SCRIPTURE
"Peace I leave with you; my peace I give to you. Not as the world gives do I give it to you. Do not let your hearts be troubled or afraid." - John 14:27

REFLECTION
Today, take a moment to reflect on the true source of peace—time spent in stillness and prayer. As busy moms, carving out even just five minutes of quiet can transform our day. Let's remember, peace isn't found in a completed to-do list or a perfect home but in the moments we connect with God in the silence of our hearts. Today, aim to find a few minutes to be still. Use this time to breathe deeply, reflect, and perhaps offer a short prayer. In these moments, we find the strength and peace to embrace the joys and challenges of motherhood with a renewed spirit.

PRAYER
Loving Father, in the midst of my busy day, help me find those precious moments of stillness where I can connect with You. Grant me the wisdom to prioritize these peaceful pauses, knowing that in Your presence I find the strength and grace I need for motherhood. Help me to remember that true peace comes not from external accomplishments, but from resting in Your love. Guide me to create space in my day for these sacred moments of connection. Amen.

POSITIVE THOUGHT OF THE DAY
I find peace in moments of stillness with God, transforming my day through His presence.

January 2nd

Thoughtful Choices for a Peaceful Day

SCRIPTURE
"I have set before you life and death, the blessing and the curse. Choose life, then, that you and your descendants may live." - Deuteronomy 30:19

REFLECTION
Reflect on your daily tasks today, not as burdens you must carry, but as choices you willingly embrace. Each task, whether it's laundry or a work assignment, represents a part of life's responsibilities that you choose to undertake for the love and care of your family and yourself. By transforming "I have to" into "I choose to," you reclaim power over your day and infuse your actions with intention and peace.

PRAYER
Gracious God, help me to see each task before me as an opportunity to choose love. Transform my perspective on daily responsibilities from burdens to blessed choices that serve my family and honor You. Give me the grace to embrace these moments with joy and purpose, knowing that each choice I make can be an expression of love. Guide me to make decisions that align with Your will and bring peace to our home. Amen.

POSITIVE THOUGHT OF THE DAY
I choose my actions with intention, finding peace in serving with love.

January 3rd

The Power of 'No'

SCRIPTURE
"Let your 'Yes' mean 'Yes,' and your 'No' mean 'No.' Anything more is from the evil one." - Matthew 5:37

REFLECTION
Today, grant yourself the permission to say 'no' to things that do not serve your highest values or bring joy to your life. Saying 'no' might feel uncomfortable, but it opens up space for the things that truly matter. Embrace this empowerment, knowing that each 'no' is a step toward a more balanced and peaceful life.

PRAYER
Lord of Wisdom, grant me the discernment to know when to say 'no' and the courage to do so with grace. Help me to set healthy boundaries that protect my time with You and my family. Remove any guilt or anxiety I may feel when declining requests that don't align with Your purpose for my life. Fill me with confidence in the choices I make, knowing they create space for what truly matters. Amen.

POSITIVE THOUGHT OF THE DAY
Each 'no' creates space for what truly matters in my life.

January 4th

Integrating Prayer into the Everyday

SCRIPTURE
"Pray without ceasing. In all circumstances give thanks, for this is the will of God for you in Christ Jesus." - 1 Thessalonians 5:17-18

REFLECTION

In the rush of daily tasks, remember that prayer doesn't always require silence and solitude. Today, let your prayers be quick whispers of hope and gratitude amidst the chaos. A simple thank you, a brief moment to acknowledge God's presence—these small acts of faith weave peace into the fabric of our busy lives.

PRAYER

Heavenly Father, help me to recognize every moment as an opportunity for prayer. Transform my daily activities into conversations with You. Whether I'm folding laundry, preparing meals, or driving carpool, let me feel Your presence and lift my thoughts to You. Thank you for being accessible in every moment of my day. Help me to cultivate a spirit of ongoing prayer in all I do. Amen.

POSITIVE THOUGHT OF THE DAY

Every moment is an opportunity to connect with God through prayer.

January 5th

Simplify to Amplify

SCRIPTURE

"Martha, Martha, you are anxious and worried about many things. There is need of only one thing." - Luke 10:41-42

REFLECTION

Today, challenge yourself to simplify your commitments. By focusing on fewer tasks at a time, you not only increase your effectiveness but also your peace of mind. Completing one task fully before moving to the next provides a sense of accomplishment and clarity that too many simultaneous tasks cannot.

PRAYER

Lord of Order, guide me in simplifying my life. Help me to discern what is essential and what can be set aside. Grant me the wisdom to focus on one thing at a time, doing it well and with full attention. Release me from the pressure to do everything at once, and help me find peace in simplicity. Thank you for showing me that less can truly be more. Amen.

POSITIVE THOUGHT OF THE DAY

In simplicity, I find clarity and peace.

January 6th

Embrace Imperfection

SCRIPTURE
"My grace is sufficient for you, for power is made perfect in weakness." - 2 Corinthians 12:9

REFLECTION
Let go of the pursuit of perfection today. Aim for progress, not perfection. Accepting a 'B-minus' in some areas of your life allows you to move forward more freely and focus on what truly adds value to your life. This acceptance brings peace by reducing the pressure to perform flawlessly.

PRAYER
Merciful God, help me embrace my imperfections as opportunities for Your grace to shine through. Release me from the burden of perfectionism and help me accept that my best effort is enough. Thank You for loving me completely, even in my weakness. Grant me the courage to move forward, knowing that Your strength is made perfect in my imperfection. Amen.

POSITIVE THOUGHT OF THE DAY
My imperfections make space for God's grace to work through me.

January 7th

Being Present

SCRIPTURE
"Be still and know that I am God." - Psalm 46:11

REFLECTION
Focus on the present moment today. Whenever you find your mind wandering to the past or future, gently bring it back to now. What is happening right now? How can you find joy and peace in the current moment? This practice will deepen your appreciation of life as it unfolds.

PRAYER
Divine Present One, help me to anchor myself in this moment, where You always dwell. When my mind wanders to past regrets or future worries, guide me back to the present. Open my eyes to the beauty and potential of each moment You give me. Thank You for Your constant presence in my here and now. Amen.

POSITIVE THOUGHT OF THE DAY
God's presence fills this moment with peace and possibility.

January 8th

Peace Through Thought

SCRIPTURE
"Finally, brothers, whatever is true, whatever is honorable, whatever is just, whatever is pure, whatever is lovely, whatever is gracious, if there is any excellence and if there is anything worthy of praise, think about these things." - Philippians 4:8

REFLECTION
Recognize today that peace is a feeling that can be accessed through your thoughts. What thoughts can you choose to think that will bring you peace? Reflect on this power you hold and use it to transform moments of stress into opportunities for calm and clarity.

PRAYER
Holy Spirit, guide my thoughts toward what is pure, lovely, and worthy of praise. Help me to recognize negative thought patterns and replace them with thoughts that bring peace and align with Your truth. Thank You for the power to choose my thoughts and the ability to find Your peace through them. Amen.

POSITIVE THOUGHT OF THE DAY
I choose thoughts that create peace and reflect God's truth.

January 9th

Learning from Failure

SCRIPTURE
"Though the righteous fall seven times, they rise again." - Proverbs 24:16

REFLECTION
Today, view each setback as an opportunity to learn and grow. Embrace failures as stepping stones to success. Each experience teaches valuable lessons that lead to wisdom and personal growth, ultimately restoring peace by reframing the concept of failure as a part of the journey, not an endpoint.

PRAYER
God of Second Chances, help me see my failures not as dead ends but as opportunities for growth. Grant me the courage to rise again when I fall, and the wisdom to learn from each mistake. Thank You for Your patient guidance and endless mercy as I navigate life's challenges. Help me find peace in knowing that setbacks are part of my journey toward Your purpose. Amen.

Every setback is a setup for a comeback with God's grace.

January 10th

Affirming Your Worthiness

SCRIPTURE
"You formed my inmost being; you knit me in my mother's womb. I praise you, because I am wonderfully made." - Psalm 139:13-14

REFLECTION
Remind yourself today of your inherent worthiness. You are enough just as you are, without needing to prove anything to anyone. This realization liberates you from the pressure of constant achievement and allows you to experience peace in being who God created you to be.

PRAYER
Creator God, thank You for making me exactly as I am. Help me to embrace my inherent worth as Your beloved child. Release me from the need to prove my value through achievements or others' approval. Let me rest in the knowledge that I am wonderfully made and deeply loved by You. Amen.

POSITIVE THOUGHT OF THE DAY
I am worthy of love and respect simply because God created me.

January 11th

Choosing Commitment Over Motivation

SCRIPTURE
"I have fought the good fight, I have finished the race, I have kept the faith." - 2 Timothy 4:7

REFLECTION
Today, reflect on the power of commitment in your journey as a mother. Unlike fleeting motivation, commitment is your anchor during challenging times. Commit to finding a few minutes each day to connect with your inner peace through silence. Even amidst the chaos of motherhood, these moments of stillness are your sacred times to renew and hear God's gentle guidance.

PRAYER
Lord of Steadfast Love, strengthen my commitment to prioritizing time with You, especially when motivation wanes. Help me to remain faithful to the practices that bring me closer to You, even during busy or difficult seasons. Thank You for Your unwavering commitment to me. Grant me the grace to mirror that faithfulness in my own life. Amen.

January 12th

The Strength in Saying No

SCRIPTURE
"Do not conform yourselves to this age but be transformed by the renewal of your mind, that you may discern what is the will of God, what is good and pleasing and perfect." - Romans 12:2

REFLECTION
Today, embrace the strength that comes from saying 'no' to things that drain your spirit and saying 'yes' to what truly matters. Each decision to say no is an affirmation of your priorities and a step towards greater peace. Remember, peace is not about pleasing everyone or filling every moment with activity, but about aligning your actions with your true values and the peace that God promises.

PRAYER
Divine Guide, grant me the wisdom to discern when to say no and the courage to follow through. Help me align my choices with Your will for my life. Free me from the need to please others at the expense of my peace and purpose. Thank You for giving me the strength to set healthy boundaries. Amen.

POSITIVE THOUGHT OF THE DAY
Each mindful 'no' is a powerful 'yes' to God's purpose for my life.

January 13th

Embrace Healing Through Clean Pain

SCRIPTURE
"He heals the brokenhearted, and binds up their wounds." - Psalm 147:3

REFLECTION
Today, reflect on the concept of 'clean pain'—the natural, necessary pain we experience as part of life. This type of pain, like the sadness of a loved one's passing or the ache of growth, is not only inevitable but also healing. It reminds us that through our trials, God shapes us, using our grief and challenges to bring about healing and growth. Let yourself feel this pain without resistance, knowing it brings you closer to the peace God promises.

REFLECTION
As a leader in your family, set clear expectations and maintain the boundaries you establish with love and firmness. Just as a manager guides their team with clear communication and supportive boundaries, so too should our parenting reflect these principles. By being a consistent and compassionate figure in your children's lives, you provide them with a sense of security and the knowledge that they are loved unconditionally. Today, lead your family not just with rules, but with a heart open to God's guidance.

PRAYER
Lord of Love, help me lead my family with both clarity and compassion. Guide me in setting boundaries that protect and nurture, while showing unconditional love. Grant me wisdom to communicate effectively and the strength to remain consistent. Thank You for showing me how to balance truth with grace in my leadership role. Amen.

POSITIVE THOUGHT OF THE DAY
I lead with love, balancing clear boundaries with genuine compassion.

January 16th

Discovering Your Intrinsic Purpose

SCRIPTURE
"Before I formed you in the womb I knew you, before you were born I dedicated you." - Jeremiah 1:5

REFLECTION
Today, embrace the profound truth that your purpose is not something to be found externally; it is already within you. You were created with intrinsic worth and purpose by God. Reflect on this: your existence itself is your first purpose. This realization can liberate you from the pressure of having to achieve to be valuable. Spend today acknowledging your inherent worth and embracing the life you are given.

PRAYER
Creator God, thank You for purposefully creating me. Help me recognize and embrace the unique purpose You've woven into my very being. Free me from the pressure to prove my worth through external achievements. Let me rest in the knowledge that my existence itself fulfills Your primary purpose for me. Guide me in living authentically as the person You created me to be. Amen.

POSITIVE THOUGHT OF THE DAY
My purpose is inherent in who God created me to be.

January 17th

Living Purposefully

SCRIPTURE
"For I know well the plans I have in mind for you, says the LORD, plans for your welfare and not for woe, so as to give you a future of hope." - Jeremiah 29:11

REFLECTION
With the understanding that you are inherently purposeful, ask yourself, "What do I want to do with my time here on Earth?" Today, let this question guide your actions and decisions. Choose to engage in activities that bring joy and fulfillment to you and others. Whether it's through your job, your role as a parent, or your hobbies, make each action a reflection of your chosen purpose.

PRAYER
Heavenly Father, guide me in living each moment with purpose and intention. Help me to recognize the opportunities You provide to make a positive impact in the lives of others. Give me clarity in my decisions and peace in my chosen path. Thank You for the gift of purpose and the ability to serve You through my daily actions. Amen.

POSITIVE THOUGHT OF THE DAY
Each moment holds purpose when lived in alignment with God's plan.

January 18th

Choosing Your Purpose Daily

SCRIPTURE
"I have called you by name: you are mine." - Isaiah 43:1

REFLECTION
Now that you know your life itself is a fulfilled purpose, consider what specific purpose you want to pursue today. It doesn't have to be monumental; it simply needs to reflect what's meaningful to you right now. This could be nurturing your children, supporting a friend, or working on a personal project. Decide what will make today purposeful for you and set out to embody that purpose fully.

PRAYER
Lord of Purpose, help me recognize and embrace the specific calling You have for me today. Guide my steps as I pursue the meaningful work You've placed before me. Give me wisdom to discern my daily purpose and the strength to fulfill it with love and dedication. Thank You for giving meaning to each new day. Amen.

POSITIVE THOUGHT OF THE DAY
I choose to live today with purpose, embracing God's calling in each moment.

January 19th

Hold Onto Your Vision

SCRIPTURE
"Write down the vision clearly upon the tablets, so that one can read it readily." - Habakkuk 2:2

REFLECTION
Today, reflect on the power of vision in bringing your dreams to life. Just as a long-held dream of getting a degree or even becoming a mom became a reality over years, your spiritual and personal aspirations can materialize through persistence and faith. Hold your vision close, nourish it with prayer and positive affirmation, and trust in God's timing to bring it to fruition. Remember, your steadfast faith and vision are the seeds from which miracles grow.

PRAYER
God of Vision, strengthen my faith as I hold onto the dreams You've placed in my heart. Help me to trust Your timing and Your ways, even when the path seems unclear. Give me patience in the waiting and courage in the pursuing. Thank You for planting holy visions within me and guiding their fulfillment. Amen.

POSITIVE THOUGHT OF THE DAY
My vision, anchored in faith, guides me toward God's promises.

January 20th

The Art of Floating

SCRIPTURE
"Come to me, all you who labor and are burdened, and I will give you rest." - Matthew 11:28

REFLECTION
In the busyness of life, it's essential to find moments to simply float—to be still and let God's currents guide you. Today, allow yourself to let go of the need to constantly do and instead just be. Whether it's a few minutes of quiet prayer, meditating on Scripture, or sitting silently in nature, embrace the peace that comes from being present and surrendering to God's flow in your life.

PRAYER
Lord of Peace, teach me the art of letting go and resting in Your presence. Help me release my need for constant activity and find peace in simply being with You. Grant me the grace to trust Your guidance and flow with Your divine current. Thank You for being my safe harbor in life's rushing waters. Amen.

POSITIVE THOUGHT OF THE DAY
I find peace in surrendering to God's gentle guidance.

January 21st

Dive Into Life

SCRIPTURE
"Be strong and courageous. Do not be afraid or terrified because of them, for the LORD your God goes with you; he will never leave you nor forsake you." - Deuteronomy 31:6

REFLECTION
Sometimes, the best way to overcome hesitation or fear is to dive right into the challenges and opportunities God places before you. Like jumping into a cold pool, the initial shock gives way to exhilaration and joy. Today, take a bold step towards a goal or challenge you've been avoiding. Trust that God is with you, and allow your faith to propel you into action.

PRAYER
God of Courage, grant me the boldness to dive into the opportunities You present. When hesitation holds me back, remind me of Your constant presence and support. Thank You for being my strength and security as I step out in faith. Help me embrace new challenges with confidence in Your guidance. Amen.

POSITIVE THOUGHT OF THE DAY
I step forward boldly, knowing God is with me in every new beginning.

January 22nd

Overcoming Negative 'What Ifs'

SCRIPTURE
"Cast your care upon the LORD, who will give you support. God will never allow the righteous to stumble." - Psalm 55:23

REFLECTION
Today, confront the 'What If' syndrome that often focuses on negative outcomes. When you catch yourself worrying about potential failures

or challenges, flip the narrative. Ask yourself, "What if everything goes right?" or "What if this challenge brings me closer to God's plan for me?" Use this shift in perspective to fuel your faith and actions, turning fear into possibility and trust in God's guidance.

PRAYER
Divine Protector, help me transform my anxious thoughts into prayers of hope and trust. When negative "what ifs" crowd my mind, guide me to see Your possibilities instead. Thank You for Your faithful presence that turns my fears into opportunities for growth. Grant me the wisdom to recognize Your hand in every situation. Amen.

POSITIVE THOUGHT OF THE DAY
I choose to see God's possibilities in every situation.

January 23rd

Embracing Positive Possibilities

SCRIPTURE
"For the Spirit God gave us does not make us timid, but gives us power, love and self-discipline." - 2 Timothy 1:7

REFLECTION
Reflect on the opportunities and dreams you've been hesitant to pursue due to fear of the unknown. Today, let the positive 'what ifs' guide your thoughts. What if your actions could lead to success, joy, and fulfillment? Imagine the best outcomes and allow these visions to motivate you to step forward in faith, trusting that God supports your journey.

PRAYER
Lord of Possibilities, open my eyes to see the positive potential in every situation. Replace my fears with faith and my doubts with determination. Thank You for the gift of imagination that allows me to envision beautiful possibilities. Help me move forward with confidence in Your guidance. Amen.

POSITIVE THOUGHT OF THE DAY
I embrace the positive possibilities God places before me.

January 24th

Learning from Every Outcome

SCRIPTURE
"We know that all things work for good for those who love God, who are called according to his purpose." - Romans 8:28

REFLECTION
Consider that every experience, whether perceived as good or bad, offers valuable lessons. What if your challenges are just hidden blessings or lessons in disguise? Today, approach every situation with openness to learn and grow. Embrace the mindset that no outcome is purely negative if it teaches you something about yourself or brings you closer to understanding God's will.

PRAYER
God of Wisdom, help me see the learning opportunity in every situation. Open my heart to receive the lessons You have for me in both successes and setbacks. Thank You for using all circumstances to shape me and draw me closer to You. Grant me the wisdom to recognize Your teaching in every experience. Amen.

POSITIVE THOUGHT OF THE DAY
Every experience brings me closer to God's purpose for my life.

January 25th

Understanding Worry as a Feeling

SCRIPTURE
"Therefore I tell you, do not worry about your life, what you will eat [or drink], or about your body, what you will wear... Can any of you by worrying add a single moment to your life-span?" - Matthew 6:25,27

REFLECTION
Today, recognize that worry is just a feeling, often sparked by your thoughts. When worries arise, take a moment to reflect on the thoughts fueling these feelings. Shift your focus to thoughts that are rooted in faith and trust in God's plan. Remind yourself that God is with you, and His grace is sufficient to handle any challenges that come your way. This shift can help reduce the intensity and duration of worry, enabling you to focus on the present blessings.

PRAYER
Prince of Peace, help me recognize worry as just a feeling that I can entrust to You. When anxious thoughts arise, guide me back to the truth of Your faithful presence and care. Thank You for Your promise to be with me in every circumstance. Grant me the peace that comes from trusting in Your provision. Amen.

POSITIVE THOUGHT OF THE DAY
My trust in God is stronger than any worry I face.

January 26th

Choosing Thoughts That Lead to Peace

SCRIPTURE
"Finally, brothers, whatever is true, whatever is honorable, whatever is just, whatever is pure, whatever is lovely, whatever is gracious, if there is any excellence and if there is anything worthy of praise, think about these things." - Philippians 4:8

REFLECTION
When worry visits, remember it is not your only option. Today, actively choose to replace worry with thoughts of peace and trust. Consider the worst that could happen, and then entrust it to God, knowing that He can bring good from any situation. This practice helps keep you grounded in the present moment, where God's peace can be most profoundly felt.

PRAYER
Loving Father, guide my thoughts toward what is good, pure, and peaceful. When worry threatens to overwhelm me, help me choose thoughts that align with Your truth and promise. Thank You for the power to select thoughts that bring peace. Show me how to focus on Your faithfulness rather than my fears. Amen.

POSITIVE THOUGHT OF THE DAY
I choose thoughts of peace and trust in God's faithfulness.

January 27th

Redirecting Worry into Action

SCRIPTURE
"Do not be anxious about anything, but in every situation, by prayer and petition, with thanksgiving, present your requests to God." - Philippians 4:6

REFLECTION
Use moments of worry as signals to take action. When you begin to worry, ask yourself what steps you can take to address the source of your worry or to prepare for potential outcomes. Taking action can often alleviate the power of worry by providing a sense of control and purpose. After taking action, release the outcome to God, trusting in His perfect timing and will.

PRAYER
God of Action, help me transform my worries into constructive steps forward. Guide me to know when to act and when to surrender outcomes to You. Thank You for giving me both the wisdom to take action and the

faith to trust in Your providence. Grant me discernment in responding to my concerns. Amen.

POSITIVE THOUGHT OF THE DAY
I transform worry into purposeful action, trusting God with the results.

January 28th

Embracing the Calm Center

SCRIPTURE
"The LORD gives strength to his people; the LORD blesses his people with peace." - Psalm 29:11

REFLECTION
Today, remind yourself that like a cyclone, your strength as a mom comes from maintaining a calm center. When life whirls around you with its challenges and busyness, focus on keeping peace within your heart and mind. Draw from this inner calm to face each situation with grace and wisdom, knowing that your stability affects not only you but also those you love.

PRAYER
Lord of Peace, help me maintain my calm center amidst life's storms. When chaos swirls around me, anchor me in Your presence and peace. Thank You for being my steady foundation in all circumstances. Help me radiate Your peace to those around me. Amen.

POSITIVE THOUGHT OF THE DAY
My calm center, rooted in God's presence, gives me strength for every challenge.

January 29th

Anchored in Faith

SCRIPTURE
"We have this hope as an anchor for the soul, firm and secure." - Hebrews 6:19

REFLECTION
Anchor your day in faith, remembering that God's presence provides a steadfast foundation when the storms of life intensify. Today, take moments to connect with God through prayer, Scripture, or quiet reflection. Trust in His promise to offer peace that surpasses all understanding, and let this peace fill you and flow from you as you navigate your day.

PRAYER
Faithful God, be my anchor in all circumstances. When life's storms threaten to overwhelm me, help me stay firmly rooted in Your presence. Thank You for being my unchanging source of strength and stability. Keep me grounded in Your truth throughout this day. Amen.

POSITIVE THOUGHT OF THE DAY
My faith in God anchors me through every storm.

January 30th

Using Awareness to Stay Centered

SCRIPTURE
"The Lord is near to all who call upon him, to all who call upon him in truth." - Psalm 145:18

REFLECTION
Utilize awareness to stay centered amidst life's chaos. Recognize when you are starting to feel overwhelmed and identify what category of your experience (circumstances, thoughts, feelings, actions, or results) you can address or adjust. By consciously choosing how you react, you can maintain your calm and continue to make decisions from a place of peace.

PRAYER
God of Wisdom, sharpen my awareness of Your presence in every moment. Help me recognize when I'm becoming overwhelmed and guide me back to Your peace. Thank You for being constantly available to center and ground me. Grant me the discernment to respond to life's challenges with conscious choice rather than reaction. Amen.

POSITIVE THOUGHT OF THE DAY
My awareness of God's presence keeps me centered and at peace.

January 31st

Letting Go of Self-Criticism

SCRIPTURE
"There is now no condemnation for those who are in Christ Jesus." - Romans 8:1

REFLECTION
Release any judgment or self-criticism when you find yourself caught in the storm instead of the calm. Remember, perfection is not the goal; resilience is. When you notice harsh self-talk or undue criticism, gently

redirect your thoughts to affirmations of your strength and capability. Embrace each experience as an opportunity to learn and grow stronger in your role as a mom.

PRAYER
Merciful Father, help me release self-criticism and embrace Your loving acceptance. When I judge myself harshly, remind me of Your grace and unconditional love. Thank You for seeing me through eyes of compassion and understanding. Guide me to view myself with the same kindness You show me. Amen.

POSITIVE THOUGHT OF THE DAY
I replace self-criticism with God's loving acceptance of who I am.

February

February 1st

The Role of Self-Awareness in Peace

SCRIPTURE
"Examine yourselves, to see whether you are in the faith. Test yourselves."
- 2 Corinthians 13:5

REFLECTION
Cultivate a practice of self-awareness by becoming the observer of your own thoughts. Today, take a few moments to reflect on your thinking patterns. Are they serving your peace and happiness, or are they detracting from it? By observing your thoughts without judgment, you create a space for choice—where you can decide to foster thoughts that align with God's peace and your wellbeing.

PRAYER
Holy Spirit, guide me in examining my thoughts with wisdom and gentleness. Help me develop greater self-awareness so I can align my thinking with Your truth. Grant me the discernment to recognize thoughts that bring peace and those that disturb it. Thank You for showing me the path to inner harmony through conscious awareness. Amen.

POSITIVE THOUGHT OF THE DAY
Through self-awareness, I choose thoughts that bring God's peace.

February 2nd

Prioritizing Your Relationships

SCRIPTURE
"But seek first his kingdom and his righteousness, and all these things will be given to you as well." - Matthew 6:33

REFLECTION
Consider the order of your key relationships today: God, yourself, your spouse, your children, extended family, community, and finally, your possessions. Reflect on whether these priorities are reflected in your daily life and how you might need to adjust to align more closely with these priorities. This reflection can help ensure that your actions and focus are in harmony with your deepest values.

PRAYER
Lord of Relationships, help me order my life according to Your divine wisdom. Guide me to prioritize what truly matters and to invest my time and energy accordingly. Show me where I need to make adjustments to

better align with Your will. Thank You for helping me create harmony in my relationships. Amen.

POSITIVE THOUGHT OF THE DAY
I align my priorities with God's order, finding peace in proper balance.

February 3rd

Using Your Brain for Spiritual Growth

SCRIPTURE
"Do not conform to the pattern of this world, but be transformed by the renewing of your mind." - Romans 12:2

REFLECTION
Begin thinking about thinking—as a spiritual exercise. Today, whenever you find yourself reacting emotionally or spiritually to a situation, pause to consider the thoughts driving those reactions. This higher level of thinking helps you identify when you're being led by the Spirit and when you're being swayed by less helpful impulses.

PRAYER
Divine Teacher, transform my thought patterns to align with Your truth. Help me recognize the difference between Spirit-led thinking and worldly reactions. Grant me wisdom to pause and reflect before responding to life's challenges. Thank You for the gift of a mind that can grow in spiritual understanding. Amen.

POSITIVE THOUGHT OF THE DAY
I grow spiritually by mindfully examining my thoughts.

February 4th

Recognizing Problems

SCRIPTURE
"The wise woman builds her house, but with her own hands the foolish one tears hers down." - Proverbs 14:1

REFLECTION
Reflect today on what challenges you face and ask yourself, "Is this even a problem?" Often, we may react to situations based on initial feelings without assessing their true impact on our lives. By questioning the problem's validity, you can determine whether it warrants concern or if it's an opportunity for growth and learning.

PRAYER
God of Wisdom, grant me discernment to distinguish between true challenges and perceived problems. Help me respond with wisdom rather than react with worry. Give me clarity to see opportunities for growth where I once saw only obstacles. Thank You for guiding my perspective. Amen.

POSITIVE THOUGHT OF THE DAY
I discern true challenges from perceived problems with God's wisdom.

February 5th

Understanding Our Problems

SCRIPTURE
"The heart of the discerning acquires knowledge, for the ears of the wise seek it out." - Proverbs 18:15

REFLECTION

If you've identified something as a problem, delve deeper by asking, "Why is this a problem?" This question helps to uncover the underlying reasons for your concerns and guides you toward a clearer understanding of what makes the situation challenging. Understanding 'why' provides the foundation for effective problem-solving and personal growth.

PRAYER
Lord of Understanding, illuminate the root causes of my concerns. Help me look beneath the surface to gain deeper insight into the challenges I face. Grant me wisdom to see beyond immediate circumstances to understand Your greater purpose. Thank You for guiding me toward greater understanding. Amen.

POSITIVE THOUGHT OF THE DAY
Understanding why leads me to wisdom and growth.

February 6th

Seeking Simple Solutions

SCRIPTURE
"For God is not a God of confusion but of peace." - 1 Corinthians 14:33

REFLECTION

When faced with a problem, ask yourself, "What is the easiest solution?" This approach encourages you to find straightforward and practical solutions, reducing stress and complexity. It reminds you that sometimes the simplest answers can lead to peace and resolution, allowing you to manage challenges with grace and efficiency.

PRAYER

God of Order, guide me toward simple solutions when I face complex problems. Help me resist the tendency to overcomplicate matters. Grant me clarity to see straightforward paths forward. Thank You for providing wisdom in solving life's challenges. Amen.

POSITIVE THOUGHT OF THE DAY

I embrace simple solutions with faith and confidence.

February 7th

Learning and Preventing Future Issues

SCRIPTURE

"The prudent see danger and take refuge, but the simple keep going and pay the penalty." - Proverbs 22:3

REFLECTION

After addressing a problem, take time to reflect on its causes and consider ways to prevent similar issues in the future. Ask, "What was the cause of this problem, and how can I prevent it in the future?" This introspective approach not only solves the current issue but also equips you with knowledge and strategies to handle future challenges, enhancing your resilience and wisdom.

PRAYER

Heavenly Father, help me learn from each challenge I face. Give me wisdom to recognize patterns and prevent future difficulties. Thank You for the lessons embedded in every trial. Guide me in applying these insights to grow stronger and wiser. Amen.

POSITIVE THOUGHT OF THE DAY

Each challenge teaches me wisdom for future growth.

February 8th

Commit to Holiness in Pursuit of Goals

SCRIPTURE
"But just as he who called you is holy, so be holy in all you do." - 1 Peter 1:15

REFLECTION
Reflect today on your commitment to your spiritual growth as you pursue your earthly goals. Let your actions not only aim for success but also for a closer relationship with God. As you set goals, consider how they align with your faith and values. Commit to making decisions that enhance your spiritual well-being, bringing you closer to holiness with each step forward.

PRAYER
Holy God, guide my pursuit of goals to reflect Your holiness. Help me align my ambitions with Your divine purpose. May each step I take draw me closer to You while advancing Your kingdom. Thank You for calling me to a life of holy purpose. Amen.

POSITIVE THOUGHT OF THE DAY
My goals align with God's call to holiness.

February 9th

Finding Joy in Commitment

SCRIPTURE
"Serve the LORD with gladness; come before him with joyful songs." - Psalm 100:2

REFLECTION
Embrace the joy that comes from steadfast commitment to your goals. When you commit wholeheartedly, each challenge becomes a testament to your faith and determination. Let this dedication bring you happiness, knowing that with God's guidance, you are capable of overcoming any obstacle. Celebrate the happiness that comes from living a life aligned with your deepest values and commitments.

PRAYER
Lord of Joy, fill my heart with gladness as I remain committed to Your path. Help me find delight in dedication and pleasure in perseverance. Thank You for the joy that comes from serving You wholeheartedly. Let my commitment be a source of celebration. Amen.

POSITIVE THOUGHT OF THE DAY
My commitment to God's path fills me with joy.

February 10th

Health Through Committed Actions

SCRIPTURE
"Do you not know that your bodies are temples of the Holy Spirit, who is in you, whom you have received from God?" - 1 Corinthians 6:19

REFLECTION
Today, focus on how commitment to your health can transform your life. Whether it's choosing nutritious foods, engaging in daily physical activity, or ensuring enough rest, let each health-focused decision be a step towards a healthier you. Honor your body as a temple of the Holy Spirit by committing to habits that enhance your physical well-being, contributing to a holistic sense of health.

PRAYER
Divine Healer, guide me in caring for the body You've given me. Help me make choices that honor Your temple. Grant me discipline to maintain healthy habits and wisdom to balance rest and activity. Thank You for the gift of physical health. Amen.

POSITIVE THOUGHT OF THE DAY
I honor God by caring for my body with committed action.

February 11th

Celebrate Spiritual and Personal Growth

SCRIPTURE
"But grow in the grace and knowledge of our Lord and Savior Jesus Christ."
- 2 Peter 3:18

REFLECTION
Take a moment today to celebrate your spiritual and personal growth, achieved through commitment to your goals. Acknowledge the divine support you've received and the inner strength you've cultivated. Celebrating these victories not only boosts your spirit but also reaffirms your commitment to a life of purpose, health, and happiness.

PRAYER
Gracious God, thank You for the growth You've fostered in my life. Help me recognize and celebrate the progress You've enabled. Fill me with

gratitude for every step forward and confidence for the journey ahead. Let my celebrations honor Your faithful guidance. Amen.

POSITIVE THOUGHT OF THE DAY
I celebrate the growth God nurtures in my life.

February 12th

Embracing Clarity in Chaos

SCRIPTURE
"For God is not a God of disorder but of peace." - 1 Corinthians 14:33

REFLECTION
In our journey toward creating a serene home and mind, understanding the link between physical clutter and mental chaos is crucial. Just as clutter represents the chaos in our minds, organizing our space can lead to a clearer, more focused state of being. Consider how the spaces you inhabit reflect the state of your mind and take intentional steps to declutter both. As you remove the unnecessary and organize what remains, reflect on how this act of tidying mirrors the cleansing of your soul, bringing you closer to the peace God promises.

PRAYER
Heavenly Father, grant me the serenity to organize my surroundings and my thoughts. Help me to see the beauty in simplicity and find your peace in the spaces I create. Guide me in clearing both physical and mental clutter, creating room for Your presence to fill every area of my life. Amen.

POSITIVE THOUGHT OF THE DAY
As I clear my space, God's peace fills my heart and mind.

February 13th

Ready for Action

SCRIPTURE
"For I am about to do something new. See, I have already begun! Do you not see it?" - Isaiah 43:19

REFLECTION
After clearing your space and mind, you're now ready for purposeful action. Today is about moving forward with intention, taking those steps you've been preparing for. Let your cleared space and organized mind propel you into meaningful activity, knowing that God has prepared you for this moment of forward motion.

PRAYER
God of New Beginnings, energize my spirit for the actions ahead. As I step forward into new possibilities, guide my movements with Your wisdom. Thank You for preparing me through the work of clearing and organizing. Help me move forward with confidence and purpose. Amen.

POSITIVE THOUGHT OF THE DAY
With a clear mind and space, I move forward in God's purpose.

February 14th

Nurturing Inner Calm

SCRIPTURE
"Peace I leave with you; my peace I give to you. Not as the world gives do I give it to you. Let not your hearts be troubled, neither let them be afraid." - John 14:27

REFLECTION
On this journey of organization and clarity, remember that the ultimate goal is inner peace. Your organized space serves as a foundation for a calm mind and spirit. Today, focus on nurturing that inner tranquility, letting it flow from your organized environment into your heart and thoughts.

PRAYER
Prince of Peace, help me cultivate and maintain inner calm amidst my daily activities. Let the order around me support the peace within me. Thank You for the gift of Your perfect peace. Guide me in maintaining this serenity in both my space and spirit. Amen.

POSITIVE THOUGHT OF THE DAY
My organized space reflects and nurtures my inner peace.

February 15th

Maintaining the Sacred Space

SCRIPTURE
"In his hand are the depths of the earth, and the mountain peaks belong to him." - Psalm 95:4

REFLECTION
Consider your organized space as sacred ground - a place where God's peace dwells. Just as we maintain sacred spaces in our churches, maintain the sacred space you've created in your home. This isn't about perfection, but about preserving the peace and order that allows God's presence to be more clearly felt in your daily life.

PRAYER
Gracious God, help me to honor the space You've helped me create. Guide me in maintaining this order as a way of honoring Your presence in my home. Thank You for dwelling with me in these organized spaces. Show me how to keep them sacred for Your glory. Amen.

POSITIVE THOUGHT OF THE DAY
I honor God by maintaining sacred order in my space.

February 16th

Creating New Rhythms

SCRIPTURE
"To everything there is a season, and a time for every purpose under heaven." - Ecclesiastes 3:1

REFLECTION
As you settle into your organized space, establish new rhythms that support continued order. Create simple routines that help maintain the clarity you've achieved. Let these new patterns become natural extensions of your day, supporting both your physical space and spiritual well-being.

PRAYER
Lord of Order, help me establish and maintain life-giving routines. Guide me in creating rhythms that support both order and peace in my home. Thank You for showing me how structure can foster freedom. Bless these new patterns of living. Amen.

POSITIVE THOUGHT OF THE DAY
My daily rhythms support lasting peace and order.

February 17th

Finding Balance

SCRIPTURE
"Let the peace of Christ rule in your hearts, since as members of one body you were called to peace." - Colossians 3:15

REFLECTION
Balance in our organized spaces doesn't mean rigid perfection. It means finding the sweet spot between order and flexibility, between structure and spontaneity. Today, focus on maintaining that balance, allowing your organized space to support rather than restrict your family's life and growth.

PRAYER
God of Balance, guide me in maintaining healthy equilibrium in my home and heart. Help me find the balance between order and flexibility that best serves my family. Thank You for showing me how to create sustainable systems. Keep me centered in Your perfect peace. Amen.

POSITIVE THOUGHT OF THE DAY
I maintain balance between order and flexibility in my home.

February 18th

Growth Through Organization

SCRIPTURE
"But everything should be done in a fitting and orderly way." - 1 Corinthians 14:40

REFLECTION
See how your organized spaces have created room for growth - both physical and spiritual. Today, reflect on how order has expanded your capacity for peace, joy, and service. Recognize how this external order has fostered internal growth and development.

PRAYER
Lord of Growth, thank You for showing me how order creates space for development. Help me continue using organization as a tool for spiritual and personal growth. Guide me in maintaining spaces that nurture positive change. Bless my ongoing journey of growth through order. Amen.

POSITIVE THOUGHT OF THE DAY
Organization creates space for my continued growth in God.

February 19th

Peaceful Productivity

SCRIPTURE
"The Lord will guide you always; he will satisfy your needs in a sun-scorched land." - Isaiah 58:11

REFLECTION
Let your organized space enhance your productivity without sacrificing peace. Today, notice how order supports efficient action while maintaining calm. Your organized environment should facilitate both doing and being, allowing you to accomplish tasks while remaining centered in God's peace.

PRAYER
Divine Guide, help me maintain productivity while staying rooted in Your peace. Show me how to use my organized space to support efficient action without losing serenity. Thank You for teaching me to balance achievement with rest. Grant me wisdom in managing my energy and resources. Amen.

POSITIVE THOUGHT OF THE DAY
My organized space supports both peace and productivity.

February 20th

Simplicity's Gifts

SCRIPTURE
"But the Lord answered her, 'Martha, Martha, you are anxious and troubled about many things.'" - Luke 10:41

REFLECTION
Embrace the gifts that simplicity brings - clarity of mind, peace of heart, and space for what truly matters. Today, appreciate how your simplified space has created room for deeper relationships, more meaningful activities, and greater spiritual awareness. Let this simplicity continue to guide your choices and actions.

PRAYER
God of Simplicity, thank You for showing me the beauty of a simplified life. Help me continue choosing what truly matters over mere accumulation. Guide me in maintaining spaces that reflect Your peaceful presence. Let simplicity draw me closer to You. Amen.

POSITIVE THOUGHT OF THE DAY
Simplicity creates space for what truly matters in my life.

February 21st

Organized for Others

SCRIPTURE
"Each of you should use whatever gift you have received to serve others." - 1 Peter 4:10

REFLECTION
Consider how your organized space enables you to better serve others. Whether hosting guests, caring for family, or supporting your community, order creates capacity for generosity and hospitality. Today, reflect on

how your organized environment can be used as a tool for blessing others.

PRAYER
Generous God, help me use my organized space as a platform for serving others. Show me how to extend hospitality and care from this foundation of order. Thank You for enabling me to bless others through the gift of organization. Guide me in using this gift for Your glory. Amen.

POSITIVE THOUGHT OF THE DAY
My organized space empowers me to serve others with love.

February 22nd

Mindful Organization

SCRIPTURE
"Set your minds on things above, not on earthly things." - Colossians 3:2

REFLECTION
Practice mindful awareness as you maintain your organized spaces. Let each act of organizing be a meditation on God's presence and provision. Today, focus on bringing consciousness to your organizing activities, seeing them as opportunities for spiritual connection rather than mere tasks.

PRAYER
Lord of Mindfulness, help me maintain awareness of Your presence as I organize and order my space. Guide me in seeing these activities as opportunities for prayer and meditation. Thank You for meeting me in these everyday moments. Keep my mind focused on Your eternal perspective. Amen.

POSITIVE THOUGHT OF THE DAY
I find spiritual connection through mindful organization.

February 23rd

Legacy of Order

SCRIPTURE
"Train up a child in the way he should go; even when he is old he will not depart from it." - Proverbs 22:6

REFLECTION
Consider the legacy of order and peace you're creating for your family. Your organized home teaches valuable lessons about stewardship, respect for space, and the connection between outer order and inner peace.

Today, reflect on how your organizational habits influence and inspire those around you.

PRAYER
Eternal God, help me create a legacy of order and peace for my family. Guide me in teaching through example the value of organized living. Thank You for the opportunity to influence future generations through these practices. Bless my efforts to create lasting positive change. Amen.

POSITIVE THOUGHT OF THE DAY
My organized living creates a positive legacy for my family.

February 24th
Seasonal Shifts

SCRIPTURE
"See, I am doing a new thing! Now it springs up; do you not perceive it?" - Isaiah 43:19

REFLECTION
As seasons change, our organizational needs shift too. Be flexible in adapting your systems to new circumstances and seasons of life. Today, assess whether your current organizational methods still serve your family's needs and be open to making adjustments as necessary.

PRAYER
God of Seasons, grant me wisdom to adapt my organizational systems as needs change. Help me remain flexible while maintaining order. Thank You for guiding me through life's different seasons. Show me how to adjust while keeping peace at the center. Amen.

POSITIVE THOUGHT OF THE DAY
I adapt my organization to serve each new season.

February 25th
Sacred Rhythms

SCRIPTURE
"He has made everything beautiful in its time." - Ecclesiastes 3:11

REFLECTION
Your daily organizational routines can become sacred rhythms, connecting you to God's presence in the ordinary. Today, view your regular tasks of maintaining order as opportunities for prayer and meditation, transforming mundane moments into sacred experiences.

PRAYER

Lord of Time, help me see the sacred in my daily organizational routines. Transform my ordinary tasks into opportunities for connection with You. Thank You for being present in every moment. Guide me in creating meaningful rhythms that honor You. Amen.

POSITIVE THOUGHT OF THE DAY

My organizational routines become sacred moments with God.

February 26th

Organizing with Grace

SCRIPTURE

"My grace is sufficient for you, for my power is made perfect in weakness." - 2 Corinthians 12:9

REFLECTION

Remember to extend grace to yourself and others in maintaining organization. Perfection isn't the goal; progress is. Today, focus on the grace-filled journey of creating and maintaining order, accepting that some days will be tidier than others.

PRAYER

God of Grace, help me maintain organization with gentleness and acceptance. When perfection tempts me, remind me of Your sufficient grace. Thank You for loving me through every messy moment. Guide me in extending this same grace to others. Amen.

POSITIVE THOUGHT OF THE DAY

I organize with grace, accepting progress over perfection.

February 27th

Clear Space, Clear Purpose

SCRIPTURE

"For God gave us a spirit not of fear but of power and love and self-control." - 2 Timothy 1:7

REFLECTION

Your organized space reflects and supports your clear sense of purpose. Today, notice how external order helps clarify your priorities and goals. Let your structured environment reinforce your focus on what truly matters in your life and faith journey.

PRAYER
Purposeful God, help me use my organized space to support my life's mission. Guide me in maintaining order that reinforces my priorities. Thank You for showing me how external structure can support internal clarity. Keep me focused on Your purposes. Amen.

POSITIVE THOUGHT OF THE DAY
My organized space reinforces my clear sense of purpose.

February 28th

Sustainable Order

SCRIPTURE
"Let us not become weary in doing good, for at the proper time we will reap a harvest if we do not give up." - Galatians 6:9

REFLECTION
Focus on creating sustainable organizational systems that will serve you long-term. Today, evaluate your routines and methods, ensuring they're realistic and maintainable. Remember that sustainable order supports lasting peace.

PRAYER
Sustaining God, help me create and maintain organizational systems that will last. Guide me in developing realistic routines that support long-term order. Thank You for giving me wisdom to build sustainable practices. Grant me perseverance in maintaining these systems. Amen.

POSITIVE THOUGHT OF THE DAY
I build sustainable systems that support lasting peace.

February 29th

Celebrating Order

SCRIPTURE
"This is the day that the Lord has made; let us rejoice and be glad in it." - Psalm 118:24

REFLECTION
Take time today to celebrate the order you've created and maintained. Acknowledge the peace it brings to your life and the ways it enables you to better serve God and others. Let gratitude fill your heart for the gift of organization and the clarity it brings to your daily living.

PRAYER
God of Joy, thank You for the gift of order in my life. Help me celebrate the peace and clarity it brings. Guide me in maintaining this blessing with a grateful heart. Let my organized space continue to be a source of joy and ministry to others. Amen.

POSITIVE THOUGHT OF THE DAY
I celebrate the gift of order and the peace it brings to my life.

March

March 1st
Embracing Simplicity

SCRIPTURE
"But let your 'Yes' be 'Yes,' and your 'No,' 'No.' For whatever is more than these comes from evil." - Matthew 5:37

REFLECTION
Embracing simplicity in your words and actions can lead to a more peaceful and focused life. This year, strive to be direct and straightforward in your communications. Avoid overcomplicating situations or your feelings. Simplicity in your intentions and actions can foster a clearer mind and a more contented heart.

PRAYER
Heavenly Father, help me to simplify my life. Let my words and actions reflect my true intentions, and help me to avoid unnecessary complexity and stress.

POSITIVE THOUGHT OF THE DAY
I find peace in moments of stillness with God, transforming my day through His presence.

March 2nd
Cultivating True Happiness

SCRIPTURE
"Rejoice in the Lord always. I will say it again: Rejoice!" - Philippians 4:4

REFLECTION
True happiness is not about constant elation but finding joy in God's presence regardless of circumstances. Embrace the notion that life includes both highs and lows, and true contentment comes from understanding that happiness is not a permanent state but a series of moments to cherish. Concentrate on creating these moments for yourself by focusing on positive thoughts and actions.

PRAYER
Heavenly Father, help me to find joy in every situation. Teach me to focus on the blessings in my life and to cultivate a heart of gratitude and joy that reflects Your love and grace.

POSITIVE THOUGHT OF THE DAY
I align my priorities with God's order, finding peace in proper balance.

March 3rd

Enhancing Physical Health

SCRIPTURE
"Do you not know that your bodies are temples of the Holy Spirit, who is in you, whom you have received from God? You are not your own;" - 1 Corinthians 6:19

REFLECTION
Physical health is a blessing and a responsibility. This year, take small, manageable steps to improve your physical well-being. Whether it's incorporating a new exercise routine, adjusting your diet, or simply stretching more often, each small change contributes to a stronger, healthier body that can better serve God's purposes.

PRAYER
Lord, grant me the strength and motivation to care for the body You have entrusted to me. Help me to make healthy choices that honor You and enhance my ability to serve those around me.

POSITIVE THOUGHT OF THE DAY
I grow spiritually by mindfully examining my thoughts.

March 4th

Deepening Spiritual Life

SCRIPTURE
"But grow in the grace and knowledge of our Lord and Savior Jesus Christ. To him be glory both now and forever! Amen." - 2 Peter 3:18

REFLECTION
Holiness is a journey of continuous growth and deepening faith. This year, aim to increase the sacred moments in your life, whether through prayer, meditation, or learning more about your faith. Dedicate time each day to connect with God, allowing these holy moments to enrich your spiritual life and draw you closer to Him.

PRAYER
Almighty God, help me to deepen my relationship with You this year. Show me how to create sacred moments each day, that I may grow in holiness and live a life that glorifies You.

POSITIVE THOUGHT OF THE DAY
I discern true challenges from perceived problems with God's wisdom.

March 5th

Sharing Holy Experiences

SCRIPTURE
"For where two or three gather in my name, there am I with them." - Matthew 18:20

REFLECTION
Sacred experiences are often more impactful when shared. This year, look for opportunities to experience holiness in community—attend church events, join a prayer group, or simply share a moment of prayer with a friend. These shared experiences can amplify the sense of sacredness and foster a deeper communal connection to faith.

PRAYER
Heavenly Father, guide me to share my spiritual journey with others. Help me to find joy and holiness not only in solitude but in the community of believers, enhancing our collective experience of Your divine presence.

POSITIVE THOUGHT OF THE DAY
I share my spiritual journey with others, deepening our collective faith.

March 6th

Embracing Daily Tasks with Grace

SCRIPTURE
"Whatever you do, work heartily, as for the Lord and not for men," - Colossians 3:23

REFLECTION
Consider your daily to-do list as more than just tasks; see them as opportunities to serve and glorify God. Each item on your list, no matter how mundane, can be an act of worship when done with a heart of gratitude and a mindset focused on serving Christ through your daily duties.

PRAYER
Lord, help me to approach each task on my list as an opportunity to serve You. Infuse my daily chores with Your grace, and let my work be a testament to Your love and goodness.

POSITIVE THOUGHT OF THE DAY
Each task becomes sacred when done with love for God.

March 7th

Reducing Overwhelm by Setting Realistic Goals

SCRIPTURE
"The plans of the diligent lead surely to abundance, but everyone who is hasty comes only to poverty." - Proverbs 21:5

REFLECTION
Overestimating what we can achieve in a single day often leads to feelings of failure and frustration. By setting more realistic goals, we can find satisfaction in our accomplishments and maintain peace of mind. Remember that it's not about how much you do, but the intention and effort behind what you do that counts.

PRAYER
Heavenly Father, grant me the wisdom to set achievable goals each day. Help me to be diligent yet realistic in my planning, that I may end each day with a sense of accomplishment and peace.

POSITIVE THOUGHT OF THE DAY
I set achievable goals that bring peace and satisfaction.

March 8th

Prioritizing What Truly Matters

SCRIPTURE
"But seek first the kingdom of God and His righteousness, and all these things will be added to you." - Matthew 6:33

REFLECTION
In the hustle of daily tasks, it's crucial to prioritize activities that align with your spiritual values and God's calling for your life. Evaluate your to-do list in light of what furthers your relationship with God and your service to others, letting less critical tasks take a lower priority.

PRAYER
Lord, help me to prioritize my life according to Your will. Show me what tasks are most important for my spiritual growth and service to others, and let me not get distracted by lesser things.

POSITIVE THOUGHT OF THE DAY
I prioritize activities that strengthen my relationship with God.

March 9th

Cultivating Contentment in Completion

SCRIPTURE
"I have learned to be content whatever the circumstances." - Philippians 4:11

REFLECTION
Cultivating contentment in our accomplishments, no matter how small, can lead to greater peace and satisfaction. Each day, aim to complete your tasks with a spirit of contentment, knowing that doing your best is enough, and trust God to handle the rest.

PRAYER
Heavenly Father, teach me to find contentment in what I am able to achieve each day. Help me to trust that my efforts, combined with Your guidance, are sufficient, and let my heart be at peace with what I accomplish.

POSITIVE THOUGHT OF THE DAY
I find contentment in doing my best and trusting God with the rest.

March 10th

Celebrating Small Accomplishments

SCRIPTURE
"Do not despise these small beginnings, for the Lord rejoices to see the work begin." - Zechariah 4:10

REFLECTION
It's easy to feel discouraged when we don't complete everything on our to-do list. Instead, focus on celebrating the tasks you do accomplish, no matter how small. This shift in perspective can lead to greater satisfaction and a more joyful spirit.

PRAYER
Gracious God, help me to recognize and celebrate the small accomplishments throughout my day. Let me find joy in the work I do and peace in the knowledge that You value even the smallest efforts.

POSITIVE THOUGHT OF THE DAY
I celebrate each small victory as a step toward God's purpose.

March 11th

Prioritizing Rest and Renewal

SCRIPTURE
"Come to me, all who labor and are heavy laden, and I will give you rest."
- Matthew 11:28

REFLECTION
In our pursuit of completing daily tasks, we often forget the importance of rest. Incorporating deliberate rest and renewal into our to-do lists can prevent burnout and refresh our souls, enabling us to serve others and God more effectively.

PRAYER
Loving God, remind me of the importance of rest in my daily life. Teach me to balance my responsibilities with times of renewal, so I may serve You and others with a rejuvenated spirit.

POSITIVE THOUGHT OF THE DAY
I honor God's gift of rest as essential to my well-being.

March 12th

Celebrating Imperfect Perfection

SCRIPTURE
"But he said to me, 'My grace is sufficient for you, for my power is made perfect in weakness.' Therefore I will boast all the more gladly about my weaknesses, so that Christ's power may rest on me." - 2 Corinthians 12:9

REFLECTION
As moms, striving for perfection can lead to exhaustion and discouragement. Embrace the concept of being 'perfectly imperfect,' recognizing that your weaknesses and imperfections are opportunities for God's strength and grace to shine through. This shift can free you from unrealistic expectations and allow you to experience greater joy and fulfillment in motherhood.

PRAYER
Merciful God, thank you for Your grace that covers my imperfections. Help me to embrace my flaws and see them as opportunities for Your strength to be displayed in my life. Teach me to rejoice in being perfectly imperfect.

POSITIVE THOUGHT OF THE DAY
I embrace my imperfections as opportunities for God's grace to shine.

March 13th

Redefining Success in Motherhood

SCRIPTURE
"Not that I have already obtained all this, or have already arrived at my goal, but I press on to take hold of that for which Christ Jesus took hold of me." - Philippians 3:12

REFLECTION
Motherhood is not about achieving perfection in every task or moment. It's about progress, learning, and growing alongside your children. Redefine success by setting realistic expectations and celebrating each step forward, no matter how small.

PRAYER
Compassionate Creator, guide me to set realistic goals in my role as a mother. Help me to see progress and effort as successes, and to cherish the journey of growth I share with my family.

POSITIVE THOUGHT OF THE DAY
I measure success by growth and progress, not perfection.

March 14th

Embracing the Messiness of Life

SCRIPTURE
"For everything there is a season, and a time for every matter under heaven." - Ecclesiastes 3:1

REFLECTION
Life, especially with children, is inherently messy and unpredictable. Rather than striving for a flawless existence, find beauty and learning in the chaos. Embrace each messy, joyous, and challenging moment as part of your unique journey through motherhood.

PRAYER
Loving Lord, help me to accept the messiness of life with grace. Allow me to find beauty and joy in the chaos, knowing that each moment is a part of Your divine plan for me and my family.

POSITIVE THOUGHT OF THE DAY
I find beauty and learning in life's messy moments.

March 15th

Anticipating Life's Demands

SCRIPTURE
"Commit to the Lord whatever you do, and he will establish your plans."
- Proverbs 16:3

REFLECTION
Planning and anticipating future demands can greatly reduce stress and anxiety. By looking ahead and preparing for upcoming tasks and responsibilities, you can manage your time more effectively and maintain a peaceful state of mind. This foresight allows you to align your daily actions with your long-term goals, ensuring that each step is taken with purpose and faith.

PRAYER
Gentle Shepherd, guide me as I plan and prepare for the days ahead. Help me to trust in Your wisdom as I anticipate my family's needs and my own, that I may manage my responsibilities with grace and peace.

POSITIVE THOUGHT OF THE DAY
I plan with purpose, trusting God to guide my steps.

March 16th

The Power of Delegation

SCRIPTURE
"Two are better than one, because they have a good return for their labor."
- Ecclesiastes 4:9

REFLECTION
Delegation is not just a task management tool; it's a way to cultivate community and share burdens. By delegating tasks, you acknowledge that you are not alone and that teamwork can bring about better results. This act can help you focus more on what truly matters, such as spending quality time with your family or nurturing your own spiritual growth.

PRAYER
Provident Creator, remind me of the strength found in community. Help me to share my burdens and accept help from others, that I may find more joy and less stress in my daily life.

POSITIVE THOUGHT OF THE DAY
I find strength in community and wisdom in sharing responsibilities.

March 17th
Embracing Automation

SCRIPTURE
"Make it your ambition to lead a quiet life: You should mind your own business and work with your hands, just as we told you." - 1 Thessalonians 4:11

REFLECTION
Automation in daily tasks can free up time and mental space, allowing you to focus more on what enriches your life spiritually and emotionally. By setting systems in place for routine tasks, you can reduce the mental clutter and find more time for prayer, reflection, and family, leading to a more fulfilling life.

PRAYER
Wise and Loving God, help me to streamline my responsibilities through wise planning and automation. Grant me the serenity to accept the things I cannot change and the courage to simplify the things I can.

POSITIVE THOUGHT OF THE DAY
I create systems that free my mind for what matters most.

March 18th
Embracing Your Identity and Dreams

SCRIPTURE
"For I know the plans I have for you, declares the Lord, plans to prosper you and not to harm you, plans to give you hope and a future." - Jeremiah 29:11

REFLECTION
Motherhood is a vital part of your identity, but it does not need to overshadow your individual dreams and aspirations. Embrace both roles by finding ways to pursue your passions while being the mom you want to be. Reflect on how the unique talents and dreams God has given you can coexist with your parenting duties.

PRAYER
Creator God, help me to see the many facets of my identity as gifts from You. Guide me in balancing my role as a mother with my personal dreams, ensuring that I live out all aspects of my life to their fullest potential.

POSITIVE THOUGHT OF THE DAY
I embrace both motherhood and personal dreams as God's gifts.

March 19th

Learning and Growing in Motherhood

SCRIPTURE
"But grow in the grace and knowledge of our Lord and Savior Jesus Christ. To him be glory both now and forever! Amen." - 2 Peter 3:18

REFLECTION
Parenting is a journey of continuous learning. No mother knows everything from the start, and that is perfectly okay. Embrace each day as an opportunity to learn something new, leaning on the wisdom of others and the guidance of God to navigate the challenges of motherhood.

PRAYER
Wise Father, thank You for the opportunity to grow through motherhood. Provide me with the resources and wisdom I need each day. Help me to rely on Your guidance and the support of others as I raise my children.

POSITIVE THOUGHT OF THE DAY
Each day brings new opportunities to grow in motherhood.

March 20th

Perfection Is Not Required

SCRIPTURE
"And we know that in all things God works for the good of those who love him, who have been called according to his purpose." - Romans 8:28

REFLECTION
The quest for perfection in motherhood is a common trap. Acknowledge that being perfectly imperfect is not only normal but expected. Your mistakes and imperfections are opportunities for growth and learning, both for you and your children.

PRAYER
Loving Lord, free me from the unrealistic expectations of perfection. Teach me to find beauty in my imperfections and to understand that every challenge is an opportunity to grow closer to You.

POSITIVE THOUGHT OF THE DAY
My imperfections create space for God's grace to work through me.

March 21st

Overcoming Procrastination with Purpose

SCRIPTURE
"Whatever your hand finds to do, do it with all your might; for there is no work or device or knowledge or wisdom in the grave where you are going." - Ecclesiastes 9:10

REFLECTION
Procrastination often stems from fear or uncertainty. It's a barrier that keeps you from fulfilling your God-given potential. Reflect on the tasks you've been delaying and consider the purpose behind them. Aligning your actions with your spiritual values can transform procrastination into proactive steps toward fulfilling God's plan for you.

PRAYER
Faithful Father, empower me to tackle the tasks I have been avoiding. Fill me with the courage and conviction to act promptly, knowing that each step I take is in pursuit of the life You have ordained for me.

POSITIVE THOUGHT OF THE DAY
I transform procrastination into purposeful action through faith.

March 22nd

Embracing Decisiveness

SCRIPTURE
"But let your 'Yes' be 'Yes,' and your 'No,' 'No.' For whatever is more than these comes from evil." - Matthew 5:37

REFLECTION
Indecision can drain your energy and waste precious moments. Being decisive isn't just about making choices quickly; it's about making them with confidence and trust in God's guidance. When you are decisive, you free up mental energy to focus on the things that truly matter—your family, your faith, and your personal growth.

PRAYER
Lord, grant me the wisdom to make decisions confidently. Help me to trust in Your guidance as I choose my paths, and protect me from the paralysis of indecision.

POSITIVE THOUGHT OF THE DAY
I make decisions with confidence, trusting in God's guidance.

March 23rd

Managing Distractions Gracefully

SCRIPTURE
"Set your minds on things above, not on earthly things." - Colossians 3:2

REFLECTION
Distractions are an inevitable part of life, especially in our digital age. However, managing these distractions by setting boundaries and prioritizing your time can help you focus on what truly matters. Consider how you can minimize interruptions to make room for peaceful reflection and meaningful interaction with your loved ones.

PRAYER
Gracious God, help me to recognize and manage the distractions in my life. Teach me to focus on the eternal and meaningful, and let my daily activities reflect my commitment to You and my family.

POSITIVE THOUGHT OF THE DAY
I manage distractions by staying focused on what truly matters.

March 24th

Shedding Guilt for Self-Love

SCRIPTURE
"There is therefore now no condemnation for those who are in Christ Jesus." - Romans 8:1

REFLECTION
Guilt often arises when moms prioritize their needs, clouding the joy of self-care with unwarranted self-reproach. Recognize that caring for yourself is not only permissible but necessary for your well-being and effectiveness as a mother. Reflect on how freeing yourself from guilt can enhance your ability to love and care for your family more fully.

PRAYER
Divine Comforter, liberate me from feelings of guilt when I take time to care for myself. Help me to understand that in loving myself, I am better equipped to love and serve those You have placed in my care.

POSITIVE THOUGHT OF THE DAY
I release guilt and embrace self-care as an act of stewardship

March 25th

Embracing Self-Care as a Divine Directive

SCRIPTURE
"Love your neighbor as yourself." - Mark 12:31

REFLECTION
This scripture not only commands love towards others but implies the necessity of self-love as its precondition. Consider self-care practices not as indulgences but as essential acts of obedience to this command. Integrate simple yet meaningful self-care routines into your daily life, recognizing these acts as foundations for a healthy, happy, and holy life.

PRAYER
Lord of Love, guide me to love myself as fervently as I love others. Show me practical ways to integrate self-care into my daily routine, affirming that caring for my well-being glorifies You and enhances my service to others.

POSITIVE THOUGHT OF THE DAY
I honor God's command to love myself as I love others.

March 26th

The Power of Positive Self-Talk

SCRIPTURE
"Finally, brothers and sisters, whatever is true, whatever is noble, whatever is right, whatever is pure, whatever is lovely, whatever is admirable—if anything is excellent or praiseworthy—think about such things." - Philippians 4:8

REFLECTION
The way you speak to yourself influences your feelings and actions more profoundly than you may realize. Transform your inner dialogue to reflect the grace and love God offers you. Replace self-criticism with affirmations of your worth and capabilities as a loving creation of God, capable of great things.

PRAYER
Creator God, help me to align my thoughts with Your truth. Teach me to focus on the positive and to speak to myself with the same love and encouragement that You speak to me, fostering a spirit of peace and self-acceptance.

POSITIVE THOUGHT OF THE DAY
My thoughts align with God's truth, fostering peace and self-acceptance.

March 27th

Daily Prayer and Meditation

SCRIPTURE
"Pray without ceasing." - 1 Thessalonians 5:17

REFLECTION
Incorporating daily prayer and meditation into your routine allows you to maintain a continual dialogue with God, nurturing your spiritual life and providing guidance for daily decisions. Start or end your day by dedicating time to reflect on Scripture, offer up your needs, and listen for God's guidance.

PRAYER
Gentle Guide, instill in me the discipline to seek You daily through prayer and meditation. May this sacred time refresh my spirit and strengthen my faith, helping me to navigate life's challenges with grace and wisdom.

POSITIVE THOUGHT OF THE DAY
I maintain an ongoing dialogue with God throughout my day.

March 28th

Service and Charity

SCRIPTURE
"As each has received a gift, use it to serve one another, as good stewards of God's varied grace." - 1 Peter 4:10

REFLECTION
Acts of service and charity are practical applications of your faith. They not only help those in need but also enrich your own spiritual journey by fostering empathy and selflessness. Consider how you can serve within your community or church, perhaps by volunteering or supporting a charitable cause.

PRAYER
Lord of Love, help me to see the opportunities for service around me. Empower me to use my gifts in ways that serve others and glorify You, building a stronger community and deepening my own spiritual commitment.

POSITIVE THOUGHT OF THE DAY
I use my gifts to serve others and glorify God.

March 29th

Reading and Studying Spiritual Texts

SCRIPTURE
"Your word is a lamp to my feet and a light to my path." - Psalm 119:105

REFLECTION
Engaging with spiritual texts can expand your understanding and inspire your faith. Whether it's studying the Bible, reading about the lives of saints, or exploring spiritual writings, these activities can provide profound insights and encourage deeper reflection on your beliefs and practices.

PRAYER
Enlightening Father, as I read and reflect on spiritual texts, illuminate my mind and heart. Help me to draw closer to You through the wisdom of Your Word and the examples of faith I study, enriching my spiritual life and guiding my daily actions.

POSITIVE THOUGHT OF THE DAY
I grow in faith through study and reflection of God's Word.

March 30th

Letting Go of Control

SCRIPTURE
"Trust in the LORD with all your heart and lean not on your own understanding." - Proverbs 3:5

REFLECTION
Embracing life's challenges often requires letting go of our desire to control every outcome. Reflect on the areas of your life where you struggle to release control. Consider how trusting in God's plan can bring peace and alleviate the stress of trying to manage everything on your own.

PRAYER
Faithful Father, help me to release my grip on the things I cannot control. Teach me to trust in Your sovereign will and to embrace the peace that comes from surrendering to Your greater wisdom.

POSITIVE THOUGHT OF THE DAY
I find peace in releasing control and trusting God's plan.

March 31st

Embracing the Present with Mindfulness

SCRIPTURE
"Be still, and know that I am God." - Psalm 46:10

REFLECTION
The practice of mindfulness—being fully present in the moment—can transform how you handle life's struggles. By focusing on the here and now, you can better discern God's presence and action in your life, reducing anxiety about the past or future.

PRAYER
Lord of Peace, anchor me firmly in the present moment. Allow me to experience each day fully, trusting that You are with me in every moment. Guide my thoughts towards a deeper appreciation of now.

POSITIVE THOUGHT OF THE DAY
I experience God's presence fully in each present moment.

April

April 1st

Cultivating Compassion and Grace

SCRIPTURE
"Therefore, as God's chosen people, holy and dearly loved, clothe yourselves with compassion, kindness, humility, gentleness and patience."
- Colossians 3:12

REFLECTION
Surrendering to struggles doesn't mean giving up, but rather giving over your worries to God and treating yourself with compassion. When faced with challenges, practice speaking to yourself with kindness and understanding, acknowledging that it's okay to seek help and support.

PRAYER
Compassionate Savior, remind me to treat myself with the same kindness and grace You show me. In moments of struggle, let me find the strength to ask for help and receive it with gratitude, reflecting Your love in my actions towards myself and others.

POSITIVE THOUGHT OF THE DAY

I treat myself with compassion and grace as God treats me.

April 2nd

Embracing Balance Over Perfection

SCRIPTURE
"For the Lord gives wisdom; from his mouth comes knowledge and understanding." - Proverbs 2:6

REFLECTION
Motherhood often sways between the extremes of feeling like everything must be perfect or fearing everything is a disaster. Recognize the beauty and peace that lie in accepting imperfection and finding a balanced approach to motherhood. Reflect on how striving for balance rather than perfection can lead to a more joyful and sustainable way of living.

PRAYER
Loving God, grant me the wisdom to seek balance in my life as a mother. Help me to understand that perfection is not the goal, but rather a harmonious balance that reflects Your grace and understanding.

POSITIVE THOUGHT OF THE DAY
I seek balance over perfection in my motherhood journey.

April 3rd

Avoiding the Traps of Comparison

SCRIPTURE
"I praise you, for I am fearfully and wonderfully made. Wonderful are your works; my soul knows it very well." - Psalm 139:14

REFLECTION
The trap of comparing oneself to others can lead to unnecessary despair and self-doubt. Embrace your unique journey and the specific path God has laid out for you and your family. Celebrate your achievements and learn from your challenges without comparing them to others'.

PRAYER
Gracious Creator, remind me daily that I am uniquely crafted by Your hands. Help me to avoid the pitfalls of comparison and embrace the path You have designed specifically for me, knowing it is perfectly tailored to my growth and Your glory.

POSITIVE THOUGHT OF THE DAY
I embrace my unique path without comparing to others.

April 4th

Nurturing Self-Compassion

SCRIPTURE
"Therefore, as God's chosen people, holy and dearly loved, clothe yourselves with compassion, kindness, humility, gentleness and patience." - Colossians 3:12

REFLECTION
Self-compassion is a vital tool in the journey of motherhood. In moments of doubt or when you feel you're swaying towards extreme feelings of inadequacy or overconfidence, remind yourself to treat your feelings with kindness and understanding. Recognize that you are doing your best and that your efforts are enough.

PRAYER
Compassionate Father, help me to treat myself with the same kindness and compassion that You show me. When I falter or doubt my abilities as a mother, let me find solace in Your unwavering love and grace, and help me to extend that grace to myself.

POSITIVE THOUGHT OF THE DAY
I extend kindness to myself as I grow in motherhood.

April 5th

Discovering God in the Ordinary

SCRIPTURE
"Be still, and know that I am God." - Psalm 46:10

REFLECTION
Often, it's in the quiet, everyday moments that we can experience profound spiritual insights. Whether it's seeing a shape in your hot chocolate or noticing the beauty in a daily routine, God often speaks through the ordinary. Encourage yourself to slow down and observe the little details of your day, for God may be speaking to you through them.

PRAYER
Creator God, open my eyes to Your presence in the ordinary moments of my life. Help me to find stillness amid the chaos, and in that stillness, let me discover Your voice and Your love in unexpected places.

POSITIVE THOUGHT OF THE DAY
I discover God's presence in life's ordinary moments.

April 6th

The Power of Quiet REFLECTION

SCRIPTURE
"In quietness and in trust shall be your strength." - Isaiah 30:15

REFLECTION
Setting aside time for quiet reflection and prayer can lead to meaningful encounters with God. Just as a simple cup of hot chocolate can become a vessel for divine communication, so too can any moment of solitude become a sanctuary for spiritual growth.

PRAYER
Gentle Whisperer, guide me to create spaces of quiet in my busy day. In these moments of solitude, speak to my heart and strengthen my spirit, that I may carry Your peace with me in all that I do.

POSITIVE THOUGHT OF THE DAY
I find strength and wisdom in moments of quiet reflection.

April 7th

Embracing Spiritual Promptings

SCRIPTURE
"And after the fire came a gentle whisper." - 1 Kings 19:12

REFLECTION
God's voice doesn't always come in grand gestures; more often, it comes as a whisper in our hearts. Encourage yourself to be open to these gentle promptings. Whether it's an urge to reach out to a friend or a sudden appreciation of your surroundings, recognize these as nudges from the Holy Spirit.

PRAYER
Lord of gentle whispers, heighten my sensitivity to Your subtle promptings. Grant me the courage to act on these divine inspirations, trusting that they lead me closer to You and to the life You envision for me.

POSITIVE THOUGHT OF THE DAY
I remain open to God's gentle whispers throughout my day.

April 8th

Affirming Your Identity

SCRIPTURE
"I am a beloved child of God, created in his image and likeness." - Inspired by Genesis 1:27

REFLECTION
In moments of self-doubt, remind yourself of your fundamental identity as a child of God. This identity is not earned by achievements or diminished by failures but is an unchangeable truth that provides a firm foundation for self-worth and purpose.

PRAYER
Dear God, remind me daily that I am Your creation, wonderfully made to reflect Your love and grace. When I doubt my worth, let me find assurance in my identity as Your child, which is enough.

POSITIVE THOUGHT OF THE DAY
I am secure in my identity as God's beloved child.

April 9th

Embracing Your Unique Role

SCRIPTURE
"I am called to be a light in the world, to share God's love and compassion with those around me." - Inspired by Matthew 5:14

REFLECTION
Each mother has a unique role that extends beyond her immediate family to influence the world with kindness, compassion, and grace. Embrace your role with confidence, knowing that God has equipped you to make a positive impact in your own special way.

PRAYER
Loving Father, empower me to embrace the unique role You have given me with courage and joy. Help me to be a light to my family and community, confidently sharing the love and compassion You have shown me.

POSITIVE THOUGHT OF THE DAY
I shine God's light through my unique gifts and calling.

April 10th

Overcoming Self-Doubt

SCRIPTURE
"I am capable of accomplishing great things through God's grace and guidance." - Inspired by Philippians 4:13

REFLECTION
Whenever you feel inadequate or doubt your abilities, remind yourself that you are capable of great things—not solely through your own strength but through the grace and guidance of God. This divine support is always available, helping you to overcome challenges and achieve your dreams.

PRAYER
Almighty God, when self-doubt shadows my spirit, remind me of Your ever-present support. Strengthen me with Your grace and guide me with Your wisdom, so I may accomplish the great tasks You have set before me with confidence and peace.

POSITIVE THOUGHT OF THE DAY
I accomplish great things through God's grace and guidance.

April 11th

Accepting Discomfort for Growth

SCRIPTURE
"I consider that our present sufferings are not worth comparing with the glory that will be revealed in us." - Romans 8:18

REFLECTION
Motherhood often involves enduring discomforts, from sleep deprivation to the emotional stress of raising children. These 'side effects' of motherhood, though challenging, are integral to the process of nurturing and teaching. Reflect on how these temporary hardships are shaping you and your children for a greater purpose.

PRAYER
Gracious God, give me strength to endure the discomforts of motherhood with grace. Help me to see each challenge as an opportunity to grow in love, patience, and wisdom, trusting that You are molding us for greater glory.

POSITIVE THOUGHT OF THE DAY
I grow stronger through embracing life's challenges.

April 12th

Finding Peace in Turbulent Times

SCRIPTURE
"Peace I leave with you; my peace I give to you. Not as the world gives do I give to you. Let not your hearts be troubled, neither let them be afraid." - John 14:27

REFLECTION
In the midst of the 'side effects' of motherhood, finding peace can seem challenging. However, peace comes not from perfect circumstances but from trusting in God's enduring presence and plan. In times of turmoil, focus on maintaining a connection to this divine peace through prayer and meditation.

PRAYER
Lord of Peace, during the tumultuous moments of parenting, remind me of Your eternal peace. Help me to anchor my heart in Your promises, finding calm amidst the storms of motherhood.

POSITIVE THOUGHT OF THE DAY
I find peace in God's presence during turbulent times.

April 13th

Embracing the Journey of Motherhood

SCRIPTURE
"Let us run with endurance the race that is set before us, looking to Jesus, the founder and perfecter of our faith." - Hebrews 12:1-2

REFLECTION
The journey of motherhood is a marathon, not a sprint. It requires endurance to face its many 'side effects.' Embrace this journey with a heart full of faith, viewing each day as a step towards fulfilling your God-given role as a mother. Draw strength from knowing that each challenge faced is a stride towards spiritual and personal growth.

PRAYER
Heavenly Father, as I navigate the enduring race of motherhood, fortify my spirit with endurance and faith. Help me to run this race with perseverance, inspired by the love and strength found in Christ.

POSITIVE THOUGHT OF THE DAY
I embrace each step of my motherhood journey with faith.

April 14th

Listening to Understand

SCRIPTURE
Know this, my beloved brothers: let every person be quick to hear, slow to speak, slow to anger;" - James 1:19

REFLECTION
Understanding your teenager involves more than just hearing their words; it requires active listening. Embrace moments of conversation with your teenager, aiming to truly understand their perspective without rushing to judgment or advice. This practice fosters deeper communication and trust, helping you guide them through their challenges with empathy.

PRAYER
Lord of Wisdom, help me to listen deeply to my child, seeing beyond words to their true needs and feelings. Grant me patience and insight to understand and support them better each day.

POSITIVE THOUGHT OF THE DAY
I listen deeply to understand and support my teenager.

April 15th

Validating Teenage Feelings

SCRIPTURE
"Bear one another's burdens, and so fulfill the law of Christ." - Galatians 6:2

REFLECTION
Teenagers often feel misunderstood or dismissed by adults, which can lead to feelings of isolation. By validating their emotions and experiences, you affirm their worth and struggles, reinforcing that they are not alone. This validation can be a powerful tool in building self-esteem and maintaining open communication.

PRAYER
Compassionate Father, teach me to validate and affirm my child's feelings. Help me bear their burdens with them, showing Your love and understanding through my actions and words.

POSITIVE THOUGHT OF THE DAY
I validate and honor my child's feelings and experiences.

April 16th

Encouraging Teen Independence

SCRIPTURE
"I have no greater joy than to hear that my children are walking in the truth." - 3 John 1:4

REFLECTION
As teenagers grow, they need more independence to explore their identities and make their own decisions. While it's challenging to step back, doing so allows them to develop responsibility and confidence. Encourage their independence by providing guidance when needed but allowing them the freedom to make choices and learn from their own experiences.

PRAYER
Gracious God, guide me in supporting my child's journey toward independence. Help me to provide them with the freedom to grow, while always being ready to guide them with Your wisdom and love.

POSITIVE THOUGHT OF THE DAY
I support my child's growth toward healthy independence.

April 17th

Embracing Emotional Growth

SCRIPTURE
"Consider it pure joy, my brothers and sisters, whenever you face trials of many kinds, because you know that the testing of your faith produces perseverance." - James 1:2-3

REFLECTION
Embracing discomfort is not about seeking out pain but about recognizing the growth that comes from enduring life's inevitable challenges. Reflect on how facing and accepting negative emotions can lead to greater resilience and a deeper understanding of both joy and sorrow.

PRAYER
Compassionate Creator, help me to see the value in every emotional experience. Grant me the courage to face discomfort with grace, knowing that each challenge is an opportunity to grow closer to You and strengthen my faith.

POSITIVE THOUGHT OF THE DAY
I find strength in facing and accepting all emotions.

April 18th

Processing Negative Emotions

SCRIPTURE
"Cast all your anxiety on him because he cares for you." - 1 Peter 5:7

REFLECTION
Learning to process negative emotions effectively is a vital skill in achieving emotional balance. When feelings of sadness, anger, or fear arise, take a moment to pause and identify these emotions without judgment. Practice describing them and understanding their source, and then release them to God in prayer.

PRAYER
Lord of Peace, teach me to process my emotions in a way that brings clarity and peace. Help me to trust that You will bear my burdens and guide me through any turmoil, turning my worries into wisdom.

POSITIVE THOUGHT OF THE DAY
I process my feelings with wisdom and trust in God.

April 19th

Finding Strength in Vulnerability

SCRIPTURE
"He gives strength to the weary and increases the power of the weak." -
Isaiah 40:29

REFLECTION
Vulnerability often feels like a weakness, but it is a profound strength.
Embrace moments of vulnerability as chances to deepen your connections
with others and with God. Understand that these moments can be
transformative, leading to greater empathy and compassion.

PRAYER
Loving God, empower me to embrace vulnerability as a source of strength.
When I feel weak, remind me that You are my fortress and that in my
weaknesses, Your strength is made perfect.

POSITIVE THOUGHT OF THE DAY
I find strength in expressing vulnerability with God.

April 20th

Recognizing God-Given Desires

SCRIPTURE
"Delight yourself in the Lord, and he will give you the desires of your
heart." - Psalm 37:4

REFLECTION
Often, the desires we feel deeply in our hearts are imprints of God's plan
for our lives. Take a moment to consider those lingering dreams and
aspirations you hold. Are they aligned with your faith and the values you
cherish? Reflect on how these desires might not only fulfill you personally
but also serve a greater purpose in God's kingdom.

PRAYER
Creator God, help me to recognize the desires You have placed in my
heart. Guide me in understanding which of these are from You and
align with my purpose in life. Instill in me the courage to pursue these
aspirations with faith and dedication.

POSITIVE THOUGHT OF THE DAY
I recognize and nurture the desires God places in my heart.

April 21st

Cultivating Your Heart's Desires

SCRIPTURE
"Commit your work to the Lord, and your plans will be established." - Proverbs 16:3

REFLECTION
Understanding that some desires take time to develop and come to fruition can be comforting and exciting. Consider what small steps you can take today to nurture and cultivate the desires God has planted in your heart. How can you prepare the soil of your life to support the growth of these dreams?

PRAYER
Loving Father, provide me with the patience and perseverance needed to nurture the desires You have placed within me. Help me to take actionable steps that align with Your will, trusting that You will help these plans flourish in Your perfect timing.

POSITIVE THOUGHT OF THE DAY
I take faithful steps toward nurturing my God-given dreams.

April 22nd

Sharing Your Dreams

SCRIPTURE
"And let us consider how to stir up one another to love and good works." - Hebrews 10:24

REFLECTION
Sharing your heart's desires can sometimes feel daunting, especially if you fear judgment or misunderstanding. Yet, expressing these dreams can lead to support and encouragement from others. Reflect on who in your life would be a supportive confidant, and consider sharing your aspirations with them as a way to affirm and advance your goals.

PRAYER
Gracious God, guide me in sharing the desires of my heart with others. Help me to find supportive and understanding friends who can encourage and help me as I pursue the dreams You have placed in my soul.

POSITIVE THOUGHT OF THE DAY
I share my aspirations with those who support my growth.

April 23rd

Letting Go of Control

SCRIPTURE
"Trust in the LORD with all your heart and lean not on your own understanding." - Proverbs 3:5

REFLECTION
Embracing life's challenges often requires letting go of our desire to control every outcome. Reflect on the areas of your life where you struggle to release control. Consider how trusting in God's plan can bring peace and alleviate the stress of trying to manage everything on your own.

PRAYER
Faithful Father, help me to release my grip on the things I cannot control. Teach me to trust in Your sovereign will and to embrace the peace that comes from surrendering to Your greater wisdom.

POSITIVE THOUGHT OF THE DAY
I release control and trust in God's perfect plan.

April 24th

Embracing the Present with Mindfulness

SCRIPTURE
"Be still, and know that I am God." - Psalm 46:10

REFLECTION
The practice of mindfulness—being fully present in the moment—can transform how you handle life's struggles. By focusing on the here and now, you can better discern God's presence and action in your life, reducing anxiety about the past or future.

PRAYER
Lord of Peace, anchor me firmly in the present moment. Allow me to experience each day fully, trusting that You are with me in every moment. Guide my thoughts towards a deeper appreciation of now.

POSITIVE THOUGHT OF THE DAY
I remain present and mindful of God's constant presence.

April 25th

Cultivating Compassion and Grace

SCRIPTURE
"Therefore, as God's chosen people, holy and dearly loved, clothe yourselves with compassion, kindness, humility, gentleness and patience."
- Colossians 3:12

REFLECTION
Surrendering to struggles doesn't mean giving up, but rather giving over your worries to God and treating yourself with compassion. When faced with challenges, practice speaking to yourself with kindness and understanding, acknowledging that it's okay to seek help and support.

PRAYER
Compassionate Savior, remind me to treat myself with the same kindness and grace You show me. In moments of struggle, let me find the strength to ask for help and receive it with gratitude, reflecting Your love in my actions towards myself and others.

POSITIVE THOUGHT OF THE DAY
I respond to challenges with compassion and grace.

April 26th

Choosing Love in Difficult Relationships

SCRIPTURE
"Above all, love each other deeply, because love covers over a multitude of sins." - 1 Peter 4:8

REFLECTION
Loving harder often means extending love to those who may not reciprocate or who challenge us the most. It involves seeing beyond a person's actions or words to their inherent worth as a child of God. Reflect on a relationship where this approach could transform tension into understanding and compassion.

PRAYER
Creator of Love, help me to love deeply those who challenge me. Grant me the strength to see beyond their actions to their inherent dignity, offering love and forgiveness as You do.

POSITIVE THOUGHT OF THE DAY
I choose love when relationships challenge me.

April 27th

Overcoming Self-Imposed Expectations

SCRIPTURE
"Do not judge, or you too will be judged." - Matthew 7:1

REFLECTION

We often carry 'manuals' of expectations for how others should behave, which can lead to disappointment and frustration. Consider how letting go of these expectations could free you to love others more fully, without condition, and to foster more genuine and peaceful relationships.

PRAYER
Gracious God, release me from the burden of my expectations for others. Help me to love them as they are, fostering peace and understanding in my relationships.

POSITIVE THOUGHT OF THE DAY
I release expectations and love others unconditionally.

April 28th

Embodying Unconditional Love

SCRIPTURE
"But love your enemies, do good to them, and lend to them without expecting to get anything back. Then your reward will be great, and you will be children of the Most High, because he is kind to the ungrateful and wicked." - Luke 6:35

REFLECTION
True love is unconditional, not based on what others do for us but on a genuine desire for their well-being. Consider how you might love more unconditionally in your daily interactions, even when it's challenging, reflecting God's endless love for us.

PRAYER
Loving Father, instill in me a heart that loves unconditionally. Help me to offer kindness and goodness even when it's difficult, mirroring Your love and compassion in all my actions.

POSITIVE THOUGHT OF THE DAY
I love without conditions, reflecting God's endless love.

April 29th

Planning with Purpose

SCRIPTURE
"The heart of man plans his way, but the Lord establishes his steps." - Proverbs 16:9

REFLECTION
Engaging in early planning can transform your summer from chaotic to intentional. Gather input from your family about their hopes for the summer and align these with practical steps that honor everyone's needs and desires, creating a summer that feels enriching and well-managed.

PRAYER
Lord of Order, guide my planning for the upcoming summer. Help me to align our family's activities with our values and Your will, ensuring a harmonious and fulfilling season for us all.

POSITIVE THOUGHT OF THE DAY
I plan with purpose and trust God's guidance.

April 30th

Stepping Into a Flexible Mindset

SCRIPTURE
"Commit your work to the Lord, and your plans will be established." - Proverbs 16:3

REFLECTION
While planning is crucial, so is flexibility. Summer often brings unexpected changes or opportunities. Cultivate a mindset that welcomes adjustments and views them as divine opportunities rather than disruptions, enabling you to enjoy the season's spontaneity fully.

PRAYER
God of Wisdom, help me to hold our summer plans loosely in my hands. Equip me to respond to unexpected changes with creativity and faith, trusting that You are weaving our summer tapestry with beauty and purpose.

POSITIVE THOUGHT OF THE DAY
I hold plans loosely, remaining open to God's direction.

May

May 1st

Setting Boundaries for Peace

SCRIPTURE
"But I say, walk by the Spirit, and you will not gratify the desires of the flesh." - Galatians 5:16

REFLECTION
Setting boundaries around digital use can be a spiritual practice, enabling you to resist the pull of constant connectivity and focus on what truly nourishes your soul. Consider establishing specific times and zones in your home where digital devices are put aside, allowing you and your family to connect more deeply with each other and God's presence.

PRAYER
Heavenly Father, grant me the wisdom to set healthy boundaries around our digital use. Help me to discern the right times to connect online and the right times to disconnect, so that my family and I may walk more closely with You.

POSITIVE THOUGHT OF THE DAY
I set healthy boundaries that create space for spiritual growth.

May 2nd

Prioritizing Quality Time

SCRIPTURE
"Look carefully then how you walk, not as unwise but as wise, making the best use of the time, because the days are evil." - Ephesians 5:15-16

REFLECTION
In the age of digital distractions, intentional quality time has become more precious. Plan device-free activities that foster genuine interaction, such as family meals, game nights, or outdoor adventures. These moments are opportunities to strengthen family bonds and create cherished memories.

PRAYER
Lord of Joy, inspire me to create meaningful family moments that are free from digital interruptions. Help us to cherish each other's presence and build lasting bonds that reflect Your love.

POSITIVE THOUGHT OF THE DAY
Today, I choose to live fully in each moment, letting go of past worries and future anxieties.

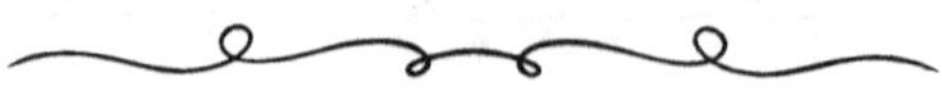

May 3rd
Cultivating Personal Growth

SCRIPTURE
"Set your minds on things that are above, not on things that are on earth."
- Colossians 3:2

REFLECTION
A digital detox isn't just about reducing screen time—it's about reclaiming time for personal growth and renewal. Use the time you'd typically spend on devices to engage in activities that enrich your soul, such as reading, praying, or pursuing a hobby. This shift can lead to a more fulfilling and peaceful life.

PRAYER
Creator God, help me to fill my time with activities that enrich and restore my soul. Encourage me to seek out and enjoy the blessings of life beyond the screen, growing closer to You and the life You desire for me.

POSITIVE THOUGHT OF THE DAY
I make intentional choices that enrich my spirit and deepen my peace.

May 4th
Understanding and Managing Guilt

SCRIPTURE
"There is therefore now no condemnation for those who are in Christ Jesus." - Romans 8:1

REFLECTION
Guilt is a common emotion for moms, often signaling discrepancies between your actions and your values. Recognize that feeling guilty is a natural part of parenting, but it's how you respond to these feelings that shapes your experience. When guilt arises, assess whether it's pointing you toward a needed change or if it's an opportunity to practice self-forgiveness.

PRAYER
Gracious God, when guilt creeps into my heart, help me discern its cause. Show me when to make amends and when to simply let go, trusting in Your mercy and understanding that You judge me not by my moments of struggle but by my heart's intentions.

POSITIVE THOUGHT OF THE DAY
I listen with love to my child's unspoken needs.

May 5th

Shifting from Guilt to Learning

SCRIPTURE
"I can do all things through him who strengthens me." - Philippians 4:13

REFLECTION
Transform guilt into a learning opportunity. Each moment of self-doubt or regret can become a stepping stone to better actions and decisions. Instead of wallowing in guilt, ask what it can teach you about your desires, boundaries, or needs, turning these insights into actions that align more closely with your values.

PRAYER
Almighty Father, empower me to use my feelings of guilt as lessons for growth. Strengthen me to move beyond self-judgment, embracing each experience as a chance to learn and to better reflect Your grace in my actions.

POSITIVE THOUGHT OF THE DAY
I equip my child to face challenges with courage and faith.

May 6th

Embracing Self-Compassion

SCRIPTURE
"As a mother comforts her child, so will I comfort you; and you will be comforted over Jerusalem." - Isaiah 66:13

REFLECTION
Self-compassion is essential, especially when navigating the challenging waters of motherhood. Treat yourself with the same kindness and understanding you would offer a dear friend. Remember, you are doing your best with the knowledge and resources you have at any given moment.

PRAYER
Compassionate Lord, teach me to be gentle with myself. Remind me that I am enough, that my efforts are valued, and that Your love is unconditional. Let me extend this same compassion to myself, freeing my heart from the weight of guilt.

POSITIVE THOUGHT OF THE DAY
I model emotional strength and grace for my child.

May 7th

Finding Peace in Routine

SCRIPTURE
"And let the peace of Christ rule in your hearts, to which indeed you were called in one body." - Colossians 3:15

REFLECTION
Daily routines, while seemingly mundane, hold the key to establishing peace and harmony in your life. Recognize the sacred in everyday tasks by setting intentions for your day that align with your spiritual and personal values. These moments of intention can transform ordinary activities into acts of mindfulness and peace.

PRAYER
Heavenly Father, guide me to find peace in my daily routines. Help me to see each task, no matter how small, as a chance to serve You and my family with love and dedication. Bless my day with Your peace as I align my actions with Your will.

POSITIVE THOUGHT OF THE DAY
I set intentions with purpose, aligning my day with God's plans.

May 8th

Balancing Motherhood with Self-Care

SCRIPTURE
"Come to me, all who labor and are heavy laden, and I will give you rest." - Matthew 11:28

REFLECTION
In the busyness of motherhood, taking time for self-care is not just beneficial; it's essential. Schedule moments for yourself to recharge, whether through prayer, reading, or simply sitting quietly. These moments of self-care provide the strength to continue caring for others with joy and patience.

PRAYER
Lord, remind me of the importance of self-care. Provide me with opportunities to rest and rejuvenate in Your presence, so I may continue to serve my family with a joyful and patient heart.

POSITIVE THOUGHT OF THE DAY
I find peace in moments of stillness and renewal.

May 9th

Embracing Each Day with Gratitude

SCRIPTURE
"Give thanks in all circumstances; for this is the will of God in Christ Jesus for you." - 1 Thessalonians 5:18

REFLECTION
Start each day with a moment of gratitude, acknowledging the blessings, big and small, that fill your life. This practice of gratitude shifts your perspective, helps you to focus on the positive, and fosters a deeper appreciation for the daily journey of motherhood.

PRAYER
Gracious God, fill my heart with gratitude for the blessings of each day. Help me to recognize Your hand in all things, and let this awareness infuse my actions with love and thankfulness.

POSITIVE THOUGHT OF THE DAY
I affirm my worth and capabilities through Christ who strengthens me.

May 10th

Handling Disappointment

SCRIPTURE
"Trust in the Lord with all your heart, and do not lean on your own understanding." - Proverbs 3:5

REFLECTION
Travel often brings unforeseen disappointments, like canceled flights or altered plans. When faced with these setbacks, it's an opportunity to practice patience and trust in God's timing, recognizing that every detour has a purpose, even if it's not immediately clear.

PRAYER
Faithful Father, help me find peace in the midst of travel disruptions. Strengthen my trust in You when plans change unexpectedly, knowing that You guide my journey.

POSITIVE THOUGHT OF THE DAY
I can face any detour with trust, knowing each leads to a new blessing.

May 11th

Embracing the Present Moment

SCRIPTURE
"Be still, and know that I am God." - Psalm 46:10

REFLECTION
Travel can be hectic, pulling us away from the joy of the moment. Consciously decide to leave distractions behind, like work emails or social media, to fully engage with the new experiences and family moments that travel brings.

PRAYER
Lord of Peace, quiet my mind and help me to fully immerse in the present, wherever I am. Let me cherish each moment with my family, finding joy in our time together.

POSITIVE THOUGHT OF THE DAY
Today, I choose to live fully in each moment, letting go of past worries and future anxieties.

May 12th

Learning from Each Journey

SCRIPTURE
"I will instruct you and teach you in the way you should go; I will counsel you with my loving eye on you." - Psalm 32:8

REFLECTION
Each travel experience, with its joys and challenges, is a lesson in disguise. Whether navigating cancellations or enjoying unexpected adventures, every experience is enriching. Reflect on what each journey teaches you about life, yourself, and your family.

PRAYER
Wise Teacher, open my eyes to the lessons each travel experience offers. Help me grow in wisdom and love through each journey's challenges and delights.

POSITIVE THOUGHT OF THE DAY
Every journey is a chapter in my story, rich with lessons and growth.

May 13th

Understanding Children's Emotional Communication

SCRIPTURE
"Understand this, my dear brothers and sisters: You must all be quick to listen, slow to speak, and slow to get angry." - James 1:19

REFLECTION
When your child displays challenging behaviors or intense emotions, it's often a form of communication. Their actions may express needs or feelings they can't articulate. Observing and listening deeply without immediate judgment allows you to understand the underlying issues and provide the support they need.

PRAYER
Heavenly Father, grant me the patience and insight to understand what my child is truly communicating through their behavior. Help me respond with wisdom and empathy, guiding them towards emotional maturity.

POSITIVE THOUGHT OF THE DAY
I listen with love to my child's unspoken needs.

May 14th

Fostering Emotional Resilience

SCRIPTURE
"Be strong and courageous. Do not be afraid or terrified because of them, for the Lord your God goes with you; he will never leave you nor forsake you." - Deuteronomy 31:6

REFLECTION
Teaching children to handle disappointment and setbacks is crucial for developing resilience. Encourage them to express their feelings and discuss their experiences openly. This guidance helps them learn to navigate life's ups and downs with confidence and faith.

PRAYER
Lord, help me to equip my child with the strength to face life's challenges. May I provide a safe space for them to grow and learn from each experience, under Your watchful care.

POSITIVE THOUGHT OF THE DAY
I equip my child to face challenges with courage and faith.

May 15th

Role Modeling Emotional Health

SCRIPTURE
"Set an example for the believers in speech, in conduct, in love, in faith, and in purity." - 1 Timothy 4:12

REFLECTION
Your own approach to managing emotions greatly influences your child. Demonstrating how to handle feelings constructively and calmly teaches them by example. When you navigate your own emotions with grace, you show them that it's possible to respond to life's challenges with strength and composure.

PRAYER
Almighty God, let my actions reflect Your grace and strength. May my handling of emotions serve as a model for my child, teaching them to live with faith and emotional intelligence.

POSITIVE THOUGHT OF THE DAY
I model emotional strength and grace for my child

May 16th

Understanding Personal Journeys

SCRIPTURE
"For my thoughts are not your thoughts, neither are your ways my ways, declares the Lord." - Isaiah 55:8

REFLECTION
Acknowledge that your spouse is on his own spiritual and personal journey, just as you are on yours. This understanding can help you see his actions and choices in a new light, fostering patience and reducing conflicts over differences.

PRAYER
Almighty God, help me recognize and respect the unique journey my husband is on. Teach me to support him with love and understanding, just as You guide and support us all.

POSITIVE THOUGHT OF THE DAY
I accept that we are both on our unique journeys, growing and learning in God's grace.

May 17th

Effective Communication

SCRIPTURE
"Let your conversation be always full of grace, seasoned with salt, so that you may know how to answer everyone." - Colossians 4:6

REFLECTION
Open and honest communication is the cornerstone of any strong relationship. Approach conversations with your husband with the intent to understand rather than to persuade or change. This mindset shift can lead to more productive and loving interactions.

PRAYER
Lord, bless our conversations with grace and understanding. Help me to listen deeply and speak kindly, that our communication may strengthen our bond.

POSITIVE THOUGHT OF THE DAY
I communicate to understand, not to change.

May 18th

Focusing on Self-Change

SCRIPTURE
"Do not conform to the pattern of this world, but be transformed by the renewing of your mind. Then you will be able to test and approve what God's will is—his good, pleasing and perfect will." - Romans 12:2

REFLECTION
While it's natural to want to change aspects of our spouses, true peace comes from focusing on our own growth and responses. By changing your own perceptions and behaviors, you influence your relationship positively, often inspiring change in others naturally.

PRAYER
Heavenly Father, empower me to focus on my own spiritual growth and emotional health. As I change my perspective, let my heart be aligned with Your will, impacting those around me in positive ways.

POSITIVE THOUGHT OF THE DAY
I lead change by changing myself.

May 19th

Reflecting on Our Emotional Responses

SCRIPTURE
"Be angry and do not sin; do not let the sun go down on your anger." - Ephesians 4:26

REFLECTION
When we encounter emotional outbursts or challenges from our children, it's crucial to reflect on our own responses. By maintaining calm and providing a stable emotional environment, we teach by example. Assess your reactions to ensure they're helping rather than exacerbating the situation.

PRAYER
Lord, help me to manage my reactions to my children's emotions wisely. Teach me to respond in ways that foster peace and understanding within our home.

POSITIVE THOUGHT OF THE DAY
I respond to my child's emotions with calmness and clarity, fostering a peaceful home.

May 20th

Teaching Emotional Vocabulary

SCRIPTURE
"A word fitly spoken is like apples of gold in settings of silver." - Proverbs 25:11

REFLECTION
Helping our children articulate their feelings is a powerful tool for emotional management. Encourage your children to express themselves by teaching them a rich vocabulary of emotion words. This not only aids them in understanding their feelings but also in communicating them effectively.

PRAYER
Heavenly Father, grant me the patience and insight to teach my children how to express their emotions clearly and healthily.

POSITIVE THOUGHT OF THE DAY
I can help my child develop a healthy emotional vocabulary to express themselves effectively.

May 21st

Supporting Emotional Resilience

SCRIPTURE
"And we rejoice in the hope of the glory of God. Not only so, but we also rejoice in our sufferings, because we know that suffering produces perseverance; perseverance, character; and character, hope." - Romans 5:2-4

REFLECTION
Building emotional resilience in our children is key to helping them navigate life's ups and downs. Support your child through their emotional challenges, encouraging them to face and grow from each experience, thereby building their character and resilience.

PRAYER
Dear God, help me support my children in developing resilience. May I guide them through their challenges with wisdom and love, helping them grow into strong, hopeful individuals.

POSITIVE THOUGHT OF THE DAY
I guide my child through emotional challenges, nurturing their growth and resilience.

May 22nd

Anchoring in Faith

SCRIPTURE
"Be still, and know that I am God." - Psalm 46:10

REFLECTION
The foundation of the Cyclone Mom Method is rooted in faith. Just as a cyclone draws power from its calm center, you too can draw strength from your spiritual core. Acknowledge and tap into your God-given power, allowing it to guide you in maintaining calm and poise amidst the daily whirlwinds of motherhood.

PRAYER
Lord, anchor me firmly in my faith. Help me to recognize and utilize the divine power You have bestowed upon me to lead a calm, controlled, and confident life as a mom.

POSITIVE THOUGHT OF THE DAY
With God's help, I am empowered by my unwavering faith to navigate the storms of motherhood

May 23rd

Embracing Your Inner Calm

SCRIPTURE
"The Lord gives strength to his people; the Lord blesses his people with peace." - Psalm 29:11

REFLECTION
Embracing your inner calm is essential for effective parenting. When challenges arise, recall that peace comes not from external circumstances but from what you hold within. Practice mindfulness and meditative prayer to nurture this inner serenity, letting it spill over into your interactions with your children

PRAYER
Heavenly Father, bless me with a peace that transcends understanding. Teach me to cultivate this calm within myself that I might reflect it in my home and to my children.

POSITIVE THOUGHT OF THE DAY
I carry a reservoir of peace that influences my home and soothes my family.

May 24th

Building Confidence through Action

SCRIPTURE
"I can do all things through Christ who strengthens me." - Philippians 4:13

REFLECTION
Confidence as a mom often comes from action—taking small, deliberate steps each day that align with your values and goals. Whether it's setting consistent boundaries, pursuing personal interests, or educating yourself on parenting techniques, each action you take builds your confidence and demonstrates your commitment to your family.

PRAYER
God of Courage, inspire me to take action daily that builds my confidence and showcases my commitment to my family. Let my deeds reflect Your strength and wisdom.

POSITIVE THOUGHT OF THE DAY
I build confidence every day through my actions, knowing they are guided by God's wisdom

May 25th

Shifting Perspectives

SCRIPTURE
"Do not conform to the pattern of this world, but be transformed by the renewing of your mind." - Romans 12:2

REFLECTION
In marital relationships, it's often not about changing the other person but about adjusting our own perspectives. When disagreements arise, try to view situations from your spouse's point of view. This shift can deepen understanding and reduce conflicts, promoting a more harmonious relationship.

PRAYER
Lord, help me to renew my mind and see situations from my husband's perspective. Grant me the wisdom to appreciate our differences and the strength to foster unity in our marriage.

POSITIVE THOUGHT OF THE DAY
I seek to understand before being understood.

May 26th

Responding with Grace

SCRIPTURE
"Let your speech always be gracious, seasoned with salt, so that you may know how you ought to answer each person." - Colossians 4:6

REFLECTION
Communication is key in any relationship. Responding with grace and thoughtfulness, even in tense moments, can turn a potential argument into a constructive discussion. Practice pausing and choosing words that reflect respect and love.

PRAYER
Heavenly Father, guide my words and reactions to reflect Your grace. Help me to communicate with my husband in ways that build up our relationship rather than tear it down.

POSITIVE THOUGHT OF THE DAY
I choose words that reflect respect and love, building bridges not walls.

May 27th

Cultivating Patience

SCRIPTURE
"Be completely humble and gentle; be patient, bearing with one another in love." - Ephesians 4:2

REFLECTION
Patience is a virtue that can transform personal interactions, especially with your spouse. Recognize that personal growth and change take time. By practicing patience, you allow space for both you and your spouse to grow together at your own pace.

PRAYER
Gracious God, infuse my heart with patience as I interact with my husband. Help us both to grow in love and understanding at the pace You have set for us.

POSITIVE THOUGHT OF THE DAY
I nurture our growth with patience, allowing us both time to flourish.

May 28th

Recognizing Unique Challenges

SCRIPTURE
"For I know the plans I have for you, declares the Lord, plans for welfare and not for evil, to give you a future and a hope." - Jeremiah 29:11

REFLECTION
Parenting a child with neurodiversity presents unique challenges that may often feel overwhelming. Recognize that God has equipped you uniquely for this journey, and each challenge is an opportunity to lean on His understanding and guidance.

PRAYER
Heavenly Father, grant me the wisdom and strength to recognize the unique challenges and gifts that come with parenting my neurodiverse child. Help me trust in Your perfect plan for us both.

POSITIVE THOUGHT OF THE DAY
I am specially equipped by God to nurture my unique child.

May 29th

Choosing Connection Over Correction

SCRIPTURE
"Above all, keep loving one another earnestly, since love covers a multitude of sins." - 1 Peter 4:8

REFLECTION
Focus on building a connection with your child that goes beyond correcting their behaviors. Understand that connection fosters security and trust, which are crucial for your child's emotional and behavioral development.

PRAYER
Lord, help me to prioritize connection with my child over correcting their every action. Let Your love guide my interactions, that we may grow in understanding and closeness.

POSITIVE THOUGHT OF THE DAY
I prioritize heartfelt connection with my child, knowing it paves the way for growth and learning.

May 30th

Seeking and Offering Forgiveness

SCRIPTURE
"Be kind and compassionate to one another, forgiving each other, just as in Christ God forgave you." - Ephesians 4:32

REFLECTION
In the journey of parenting a difficult child, seek forgiveness for the moments when patience wears thin, and offer the same forgiveness to your child when they struggle. This mutual grace strengthens your bond and mirrors the forgiveness Christ offers us all.

PRAYER
Merciful God, teach me to freely give and seek forgiveness within my family. May our relationship be strengthened by the grace and forgiveness that reflects Your love for us.

POSITIVE THOUGHT OF THE DAY
I freely extend and seek forgiveness, nurturing a home of grace and understanding.

May 31st

Finding Strength in Community

SCRIPTURE
"Two are better than one, because they have a good reward for their toil. For if they fall, one will lift up his fellow. But woe to him who is alone when he falls and has not another to lift him up!" - Ecclesiastes 4:9-10

REFLECTION
Don't journey alone in parenting your neurodiverse child. Seek support from communities and groups that understand your challenges. Sharing experiences and resources can uplift you and provide new perspectives and strategies.

PRAYER
Gracious Lord, lead me to a community where I can both give and receive support. Help me find strength in the fellowship of others who understand the unique path of parenting a neurodiverse child.

POSITIVE THOUGHT OF THE DAY
I find strength and insight in a community of those who understand and support our journey.

June

June 1st

Understanding 'Yes' in PRAYER

SCRIPTURE
"Ask, and it will be given to you; seek, and you will find; knock, and the door will be opened to you." - Matthew 7:7

REFLECTION
When you feel a deep sense of peace about a decision or direction, it might be God's affirmation through a 'Yes.' Remember, a 'Yes' can still require effort and persistence from you; it's not always an easy path, but one that God has prepared you to walk with faith.

PRAYER
Lord, thank You for the 'Yes' answers in my prayers. Help me to recognize and act upon these affirmations with courage and commitment, trusting that You have equipped me for the challenges ahead.

POSITIVE THOUGHT OF THE DAY
I am equipped and empowered by God's affirmations to pursue my path with faith.

June 2nd

When God Says 'No'

SCRIPTURE
"For my thoughts are not your thoughts, neither are your ways my ways, declares the Lord." - Isaiah 55:8

REFLECTION
A 'No' from God, while often disappointing, redirects you towards something better. God's rejections are His protections, shielding you from less than His best. Reflect on the 'No's you've encountered and look for the hidden blessings and redirections they've brought.

PRAYER
Heavenly Father, grant me the grace to accept Your 'No' as a divine redirection to a path filled with greater blessings. Help me see the protection in these denials and trust more deeply in Your plan.

POSITIVE THOUGHT OF THE DAY
I trust that every 'No' from God guides me to His best for my life.

June 3rd

Embracing God's Timing

SCRIPTURE
"Wait for the Lord; be strong and take heart and wait for the Lord." - Psalm 27:14

REFLECTION
The answer 'Wait' tests our patience but also builds our faith. Waiting is not a passive state; it's a time to prepare, grow, and align more closely with God's will. Consider what God might be teaching you in this period of waiting and how you can grow stronger in your faith.

PRAYER
Lord, help me to embrace the waiting periods with faith and patience. Teach me what I need to learn and prepare me for what lies ahead, knowing that Your timing is perfect.

POSITIVE THOUGHT OF THE DAY
I grow in faith and strength as I wait on God's perfect timing.

June 4th

Interpreting Unclear Answers

SCRIPTURE
"The Lord will guide you always; he will satisfy your needs in a sun-scorched land and will strengthen your frame. You will be like a well-watered garden, like a spring whose waters never fail." - Isaiah 58:11

REFLECTION
Sometimes, the answers to our prayers are not clear-cut. This uncertainty can be a call to deepen our relationship with God, seeking closer communion and clearer understanding through prayer, scripture, and reflection.

PRAYER
Almighty God, in times of uncertainty, draw me closer to You. Enhance my understanding and deepen my faith as I seek clarity in my prayers.

POSITIVE THOUGHT OF THE DAY
I seek clarity and understanding through a deeper relationship with God.

June 5th

Starting Small with Organization

SCRIPTURE
"Whoever can be trusted with very little can also be trusted with much..."
- Luke 16:10

REFLECTION
The journey to organizing your life doesn't have to start with grand gestures. Begin with something small, like a drawer or a shelf. This manageable approach reduces overwhelm and builds your confidence in your ability to create order.

PRAYER
Lord, guide me to start small in my efforts to organize. Help me see the value in each small step I take towards a more structured life.

POSITIVE THOUGHT OF THE DAY
I find joy and accomplishment in small beginnings.

June 6th

Decluttering as a Form of Self-Care

SCRIPTURE
"But everything should be done in a fitting and orderly way." - 1 Corinthians 14:40

REFLECTION
Decluttering is not just about creating physical space; it's about making room in your life for more peace and joy. See it as an act of self-care that benefits your mental and emotional well-being.

PRAYER
Heavenly Father, help me to understand that decluttering my space is a way of caring for myself. Bless my efforts to create a peaceful and joyful environment.

POSITIVE THOUGHT OF THE DAY
I care for my well-being by clearing the clutter in my life.

June 7th

The Power of a Simplified Space

SCRIPTURE
"For God is not a God of disorder but of peace." - 1 Corinthians 14:33

REFLECTION
Embrace the power of a simplified space. An orderly environment can lead to a clearer mind and a more focused spirit, making it easier to engage with your family and your faith.

PRAYER
God of peace, grant me the strength to simplify my surroundings. Let this physical order reflect into my mental and spiritual life.

POSITIVE THOUGHT OF THE DAY
I embrace simplicity for a clearer mind and a focused spirit."

June 8th

Sustaining Organizational Habits

SCRIPTURE
"Let us not become weary in doing good, for at the proper time we will reap a harvest if we do not give up." - Galatians 6:9

REFLECTION
Maintaining organization is a continuous effort. Encourage yourself to sustain these habits by regularly reflecting on how much more peaceful your life feels with these changes.

PRAYER
Sustain me, Lord, in my efforts to keep my space organized. Help me to not grow weary but to continually find motivation in the peace it brings to my life.

POSITIVE THOUGHT OF THE DAY
I maintain my peace by sustaining my organizational habits.

June 9th

Setting Your Life's Mission

SCRIPTURE
"For I know the plans I have for you, declares the Lord, plans to prosper you and not to harm you, plans to give you hope and a future." - Jeremiah 29:11

REFLECTION
Just as a CEO crafts a mission statement to define the direction of a company, consider defining your own life's mission. This statement can guide your decisions and align your daily actions with your spiritual and personal values.

PRAYER
Heavenly Father, inspire me to craft a personal mission statement that reflects Your will and guides my actions and choices. Help me live each day with purpose and intention

POSITIVE THOUGHT OF THE DAY
I lead my life with a mission that reflects my deepest values and God's plan for me.

June 10th

Cultivating Your Environment

SCRIPTURE
"Let all that you do be done in love." - 1 Corinthians 16:14

REFLECTION
A CEO nurtures a positive company culture. Similarly, foster an environment in your home where love, respect, and mutual support are paramount. This nurturing setting allows each family member, including yourself, to thrive.

PRAYER
Lord, help me to create a home environment that nurtures growth and love. May our home be a sanctuary of peace and encouragement for all.

POSITIVE THOUGHT OF THE DAY
I cultivate a home environment where each member feels loved, valued, and supported.

June 11th

Leading with Intention

SCRIPTURE
"But the fruit of the Spirit is love, joy, peace, forbearance, kindness, goodness, faithfulness, gentleness, and self-control." - Galatians 5:22-23

REFLECTION
Embrace the role of a leader in your family by intentionally setting goals and benchmarks for yourself and your loved ones. Like a CEO, your leadership can drive your family towards collective and individual successes.

PRAYER
Almighty God, grant me the wisdom to lead my family with intention and grace. Help me set goals that foster our collective spiritual growth and personal development.

POSITIVE THOUGHT OF THE DAY
I lead my family with clear goals that promote our growth and well-being

June 12th

Accountability and Adaptability

SCRIPTURE
"Commit to the Lord whatever you do, and he will establish your plans."
- Proverbs 16:3

REFLECTION
As a CEO remains accountable to a board, stay accountable to your values and to God. Embrace adaptability by reassessing and adjusting your strategies to meet the evolving needs of your family and your personal growth.

PRAYER
Gracious God, help me remain accountable to my commitments and open to Your guidance. Enable me to adapt wisely to life's changes and challenges.

POSITIVE THOUGHT OF THE DAY
I remain adaptable and accountable, aligning my actions with God's guidance and my family's needs.

June 13th

Embracing Your Unique Journey

SCRIPTURE
"But let each one test his own work, and then his reason to boast will be in himself alone and not in his neighbor." - Galatians 6:4

REFLECTION
Motherhood is a unique journey for each woman. It's essential to focus on your path and strengths rather than comparing yourself to others. Embrace your individual experiences, learning to appreciate the unique challenges and joys your family brings.

PRAYER
Heavenly Father, help me to appreciate the unique path You have laid out for me and my family. Give me the strength to focus on our blessings and challenges without comparing our journey to others'.

POSITIVE THOUGHT OF THE DAY
I celebrate my unique journey and the lessons it brings."

June 14th

Staying Anchored in Faith

SCRIPTURE
"Cast all your anxiety on him because he cares for you." - 1 Peter 5:7

REFLECTION
In the whirlwind of motherhood, it's easy to feel overwhelmed. Remember to anchor yourself in faith. Hand over your worries and stresses to God and trust in His guidance and provision. This spiritual grounding can bring immense peace and clarity.

PRAYER
Lord, I place all my worries and challenges at Your feet. Guide me with Your wisdom and comfort me with Your peace as I navigate the complexities of motherhood.

POSITIVE THOUGHT OF THE DAY
I am grounded in my faith, which brings peace to my mothering

June 15th

The Power of Pause

SCRIPTURE
"Be still, and know that I am God." - Psalm 46:10

REFLECTION
Taking moments to pause throughout your day can be incredibly powerful. Use these pauses to breathe, reflect, and connect with God. These brief stops can help you regain your composure and perspective, enhancing your reactions and decisions.

PRAYER
God of Peace, remind me to take moments to pause and reconnect with You throughout my day. Let these pauses be times of renewal and clarity.

POSITIVE THOUGHT OF THE DAY
I find strength and clarity in moments of pause, reconnecting with God's purpose for me.

June 16th

Accepting and Growing Through Challenges

SCRIPTURE
"Consider it pure joy, my brothers and sisters, whenever you face trials of many kinds, because you know that the testing of your faith produces perseverance." - James 1:2-3

REFLECTION
Challenges in motherhood are not just obstacles; they are opportunities for growth and deepening faith. Embrace these moments as chances to learn and strengthen your character. The trials you overcome today prepare you for future joys and successes.

PRAYER
Heavenly Father, help me to see the challenges I face as opportunities for growth. Strengthen my faith and character through each trial, and let me find joy in overcoming them.

POSITIVE THOUGHT OF THE DAY
I grow stronger and more resilient through each challenge I face in motherhood.

June 17th

Setting Intentions

SCRIPTURE
"Commit to the Lord whatever you do, and he will establish your plans."
- Proverbs 16:3

REFLECTION
Begin each day by setting clear intentions. Before you even leave your bed, take a moment to decide what you hope to achieve or how you wish to behave throughout the day. This morning ritual of setting intentions can help steer your actions and mindset in a positive direction.

PRAYER
Father, as I start my day, help me set intentions that align with Your will. May my thoughts and actions reflect the goals I set and lead me closer to You.

POSITIVE THOUGHT OF THE DAY
I set my intentions with purpose, aligning my day with God's plans.

June 18th

Embracing Quiet Moments

SCRIPTURE
"In quietness and trust is your strength." - Isaiah 30:15

REFLECTION
Whether it's five minutes of solitude before the day begins or a quiet moment with a cup of coffee, embracing these brief periods of calm can significantly impact your emotional and mental well-being. These moments offer a chance to center yourself and connect with God before the day's demands take hold.

PRAYER
Lord, in my quiet moments, let me find strength and peace. Remind me to seek these times of solitude to refresh my spirit and renew my focus.

POSITIVE THOUGHT OF THE DAY
I find strength and clarity in my moments of quiet, connecting deeply with God's peace.

June 19th

Positive Affirmations

SCRIPTURE
"I praise you, for I am fearfully and wonderfully made." - Psalm 139:14

REFLECTION
Positive affirmations can shape our thoughts and feelings throughout the day. As you prepare for the day, affirm your worth and capabilities through Christ who strengthens you. These affirmations can build confidence and a positive mindset.

PRAYER
Heavenly Father, let Your truth anchor my thoughts as I affirm my identity in You. Help me to remember that I am capable and loved, no matter the challenges I face.

POSITIVE THOUGHT OF THE DAY
I am guided by God's grace and equipped for today's challenges.

June 20th

Trusting God's Plan

SCRIPTURE
"Trust in the Lord with all your heart and lean not on your own understanding." - Proverbs 3:5

REFLECTION
Some mornings may not go as planned, but trusting in God's plan can bring peace amidst the chaos. When the morning rush feels overwhelming, pause and remind yourself that God is with you, guiding your steps and adjusting your path as needed.

PRAYER
God of Peace, when my plans falter, help me to trust in Your perfect plan. Give me the peace to accept the things I cannot control and the courage to continue with grace.

POSITIVE THOUGHT OF THE DAY
I trust in God's perfect plan for my day, finding peace in His divine adjustments.

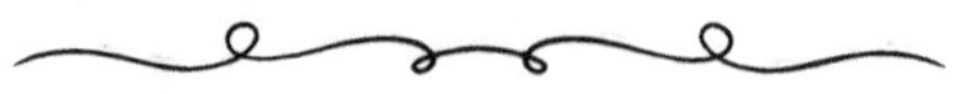

June 21st

Recognizing God's Role in Motherhood

SCRIPTURE
"Children are a heritage from the Lord, offspring a reward from him." - Psalm 127:3

REFLECTION
Motherhood, with its challenges and joys, is a divine assignment. Recognize that each day as a mother is shaped by God's hand, and your role is not just about raising children but fulfilling a God-given mission.

PRAYER
Heavenly Father, remind me daily that my role as a mother is a sacred calling from You. Help me to see my daily tasks through the lens of Your divine purpose.

POSITIVE THOUGHT OF THE DAY
I am fulfilling a God-given mission in my motherhood.

June 22nd

Seeking Wisdom in Parenthood

SCRIPTURE
"If any of you lacks wisdom, you should ask God, who gives generously to all without finding fault, and it will be given to you." - James 1:5

REFLECTION
In the busyness of parenting, seeking God's wisdom can provide the guidance and patience needed to handle every situation, from discipline to love, with grace.

PRAYER
Lord, grant me wisdom in my parenting. Let my actions and words to my children reflect Your love and guidance.

POSITIVE THOUGHT OF THE DAY
I seek and receive God's wisdom for each parenting challenge.

June 23rd

Embracing Each Day's Lessons

SCRIPTURE
"This is the day the Lord has made; we will rejoice and be glad in it." - Psalm 118:24

REFLECTION
Each day brings new lessons and opportunities for growth, both for you and your children. Embrace these daily lessons with a heart open to learning and a spirit ready to adapt.

PRAYER
Dear God, help me embrace the lessons of each day with joy and openness. Teach me and my children through our daily experiences.

POSITIVE THOUGHT OF THE DAY
I embrace today's lessons and grow alongside my children.

June 24th

Cultivating Peace in Chaos

SCRIPTURE
"Peace I leave with you; my peace I give you. I do not give to you as the world gives. Do not let your hearts be troubled and do not be afraid." - John 14:27

REFLECTION
Motherhood often feels chaotic, but cultivating a sense of inner peace can transform how you respond to daily pressures. Finding moments for prayer and reflection can center your heart and mind in God's peace.

PRAYER
Heavenly Father, infuse my days with Your peace. Help me find calm within the chaos of motherhood, anchoring my heart in Your serenity.

POSITIVE THOUGHT OF THE DAY
I carry God's peace within me, transforming chaos into calm.

June 25th

Staying in Your Own Lane

SCRIPTURE
"But let each one test his own work, and then his reason to boast will be in himself alone and not in his neighbor." - Galatians 6:4

REFLECTION
Focusing on your own journey rather than comparing it to others can significantly reduce feelings of inadequacy and despair. Recognize the unique path God has designed for you and your family, and find joy in the personal progress and distinct rhythm of your household.

PRAYER
Heavenly Father, help me to focus on the blessings and challenges of my own life, avoiding the pitfalls of comparison. Grant me the wisdom to appreciate the unique journey You have laid out for me and my family.

POSITIVE THOUGHT OF THE DAY
I celebrate my unique journey, guided by God's hand.

June 26th

Placing Everything in God's Hands

SCRIPTURE
"Cast all your anxiety on him because he cares for you." - 1 Peter 5:7

REFLECTION
Surrendering your worries and challenges to God can bring immense relief and perspective. Recognize that you are not alone in your parenting journey—God is with you, ready to share the load and provide strength when you need it most.

PRAYER
Almighty God, I place my burdens in Your capable hands. Help me to trust in Your providence and feel the weight of my worries lessen as I rely more on You.

POSITIVE THOUGHT OF THE DAY
I trust God to lighten my load and guide my steps.

June 27th

Accepting and Growing Through Hardships

SCRIPTURE
More than that, we rejoice in our sufferings, knowing that suffering produces endurance, and endurance produces character, and character produces hope." - Romans 5:3-4

REFLECTION
Embrace the challenges of motherhood as opportunities for growth and spiritual enrichment. Each difficulty teaches resilience and strengthens your character, aligning you more closely with Christ's example of perseverance and faith.

PRAYER
Lord Jesus, in my moments of struggle, remind me that each challenge is an opportunity to grow closer to You. Help me to embrace hardships with grace, knowing they are forming me into the person You desire me to be.

POSITIVE THOUGHT OF THE DAY
Every challenge is a stepping stone to greater resilience and deeper faith.

June 28th

I Can Do All Things Through Christ Who Strengthens Me

SCRIPTURE
"I can do all things through him who strengthens me." - Philippians 4:13

REFLECTION
This thought reminds us that no matter the challenge, from balancing work and home life to managing personal stress, we have a divine ally in Christ who provides strength and resilience.

PRAYER
Lord Jesus, remind me that with Your strength, I can face any challenge. Help me to draw upon Your endless power when I feel overwhelmed and underprepared.

POSITIVE THOUGHT OF THE DAY
Through Christ, I am empowered to overcome any obstacle.

June 29th

If God is for Me, Who Can Be Against Me?

SCRIPTURE
"If God is for us, who can be against us?" - Romans 8:31

REFLECTION
This powerful affirmation encourages you to view every difficulty through the lens of divine support. It reaffirms that with God on your side, no adversity is too great to handle.

PRAYER
Heavenly Father, fortify my spirit with the knowledge that You are with me in all things. Let this assurance dissolve my fears and bolster my courage.

POSITIVE THOUGHT OF THE DAY
With God on my side, I am unstoppable.

June 30th

This Too Shall Pass

SCRIPTURE
"We are afflicted in every way, but not crushed; perplexed, but not driven to despair." - 2 Corinthians 4:8

REFLECTION
Life's challenges are transient. This thought serves as a reminder that just as joyous moments pass, so too do times of struggle. Embracing this cyclical nature of life can bring peace during tumultuous times.

PRAYER
Almighty God, in moments of overwhelm, help me to remember that this too shall pass. Grant me patience and peace as I navigate life's highs and lows.

POSITIVE THOUGHT OF THE DAY
Each challenge is temporary; I find strength in knowing peace awaits.

July

July 1st

Embracing a Solution-Seeking Heart

SCRIPTURE
"Ask and it will be given to you; seek and you will find; knock and the door will be opened to you." - Matthew 7:7

REFLECTION
Today, notice how often you find yourself saying "if only" in your thoughts and prayers. Instead of dwelling in wishful thinking, transform these moments into opportunities for growth by asking "how can I?" This shift aligns beautifully with our faith, as it moves us from passive waiting to active trust in God's guidance. When we seek solutions rather than dwell on obstacles, we open ourselves to seeing God's provision in unexpected ways.

PRAYER
Lord of Wisdom, help me transform my "if only" thoughts into "how can I" actions. Guide me to see possibilities where I once saw obstacles. Grant me the courage to seek solutions and the wisdom to trust in Your guidance. Thank You for showing me new ways forward when I feel stuck. Amen.

POSITIVE THOUGHT OF THE DAY
I transform challenges into opportunities through faith-filled action.

July 2nd

Finding Peace Through Proactive Faith

SCRIPTURE
"For God did not give us a spirit of timidity but one of power, love, and self-discipline." - 2 Timothy 1:7

REFLECTION
Just as a laser focuses its light in one direction for maximum impact, our minds work best when directed toward solutions rather than problems. Today, practice shifting from "if only" thinking to asking empowering "how" questions. Instead of saying "if only I had more time," ask yourself "how can I use the time I have more meaningfully?" This mental shift opens doors to creative solutions and deeper trust in God's providence.

PRAYER
Divine Guide, help me focus my thoughts on possibilities rather than limitations. Transform my doubts into determination and my wishes into purposeful questions. Thank You for giving me a spirit of power and love that enables me to seek solutions rather than dwell on problems. Amen.

POSITIVE THOUGHT OF THE DAY
I focus my mind on solutions, trusting in God's guidance.

July 3rd

Growing in Gratitude and Grace

SCRIPTURE
"Give thanks in all circumstances; for this is God's will for you in Christ Jesus." - 1 Thessalonians 5:18

REFLECTION
A solution-focused mindset begins with gratitude for our present circumstances. Rather than lamenting what's missing, acknowledge the abundance already present in your life. When challenges arise, instead of thinking "if only things were different," ask "how can I work with what God has already provided?" This perspective shift helps us recognize God's presence in our current situation while actively seeking His guidance for growth.

PRAYER
Gracious Father, open my eyes to see the blessings in my present circumstances. Help me to build upon what You have already provided rather than focusing on what seems to be missing. Guide me to transform my moments of doubt into opportunities for growth and deeper trust in Your provision. Amen.

POSITIVE THOUGHT OF THE DAY
I build upon my blessings with gratitude and trust in God's plan.

July 4th

Embracing Daily Grace

SCRIPTURE
"Give us this day our daily bread." - Matthew 6:11

REFLECTION
Just as God provided manna one day at a time to His people, He offers us grace sufficient for each day's challenges. Today, recognize that when we try to gather tomorrow's grace for today's worries, we miss the beauty and provision of the present moment. Each sunrise brings fresh mercy and new strength for that day alone. Focus on receiving and living in today's portion of grace.

PRAYER
Provider God, help me trust in Your daily provision of grace. Teach me to gather today's portion with gratitude, knowing tomorrow will bring its own supply. Thank You for giving me exactly what I need for this day. Grant me the wisdom to stay present in Your care. Amen.

POSITIVE THOUGHT OF THE DAY
I receive God's grace fresh each morning, sufficient for today.

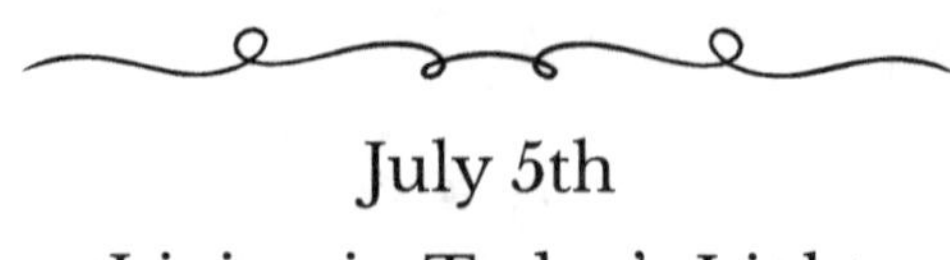

July 5th
Living in Today's Light

SCRIPTURE
"Therefore do not worry about tomorrow, for tomorrow will worry about itself. Each day has enough trouble of its own." - Matthew 6:34

REFLECTION
Consider how worry about tomorrow dims the light of today's joys. When we focus on future concerns, we miss the sacred moments before us—a child's laughter, a quiet cup of coffee, a moment of connection. Practice returning to the present moment whenever you notice your thoughts drifting to tomorrow's concerns. Each day carries its own sacred purpose and presence.

PRAYER
Lord of Peace, guide me back to the present moment when worry pulls me toward tomorrow. Help me find You in today's simple gifts and small graces. Thank You for the gift of this day, with all its opportunities to trust and grow in Your love. Amen.

POSITIVE THOUGHT OF THE DAY
I choose to live fully in today's moments, trusting tomorrow to God.

July 6th
Breaking Free from Tomorrow's Chains

SCRIPTURE
"Cast all your anxiety on him because he cares for you." - 1 Peter 5:7

REFLECTION
When we carry tomorrow's burdens today, we wear ourselves down with weight we weren't meant to bear. Like a garden that needs daily tending, focus your energy on what you can nurture and influence today. Release the habit of mental time travel that leads to worry, and instead root yourself in the present moments where grace abounds.

PRAYER
Heavenly Father, free me from the chains of tomorrow's worries. When anxiety about the future creeps in, help me cast those cares upon You. Thank You for Your constant care and presence. Strengthen my trust in Your faithful provision for each new day. Amen.

POSITIVE THOUGHT OF THE DAY
I release tomorrow's worries, embracing today's peace.

July 7th

Building Sacred Rhythms

SCRIPTURE
"But seek first his kingdom and his righteousness, and all these things will be given to you as well." - Matthew 6:33

REFLECTION
Just as water shapes stone through constant drops, our daily faithful actions shape our spiritual life. Small, steady steps in faith matter more than occasional grand gestures. Today, consider what spiritual practices you can commit to regularly—whether it's morning prayer, gratitude journaling, or sacred reading. These consistent actions create a foundation for lasting peace and deeper connection with God.

PRAYER
Lord of Constancy, guide me in establishing faithful rhythms that draw me closer to You. Help me build habits that honor You and nurture my spirit. Thank You for Your steady presence that anchors my days. Grant me perseverance in these sacred practices. Amen.

POSITIVE THOUGHT OF THE DAY
My faithful daily actions create lasting spiritual growth.

July 8th

Growing Through Small Steps

SCRIPTURE
"He who is faithful in a very little is faithful also in much." - Luke 16:10

REFLECTION
The path to transformation lies not in dramatic changes but in small, faithful steps taken consistently. Whether it's dedicating ten minutes to prayer, sharing a meaningful conversation with your child, or maintaining a peaceful bedtime routine, these seemingly minor actions build a foundation for lasting joy and peace in your home.

PRAYER
Divine Guide, help me value the power of small, consistent actions. Give me the wisdom to recognize that each faithful step matters. Thank You for showing me that transformation comes through steady dedication. Keep me focused on the daily practices that bring me closer to Your vision for my life. Amen.

POSITIVE THOUGHT OF THE DAY
I trust in the power of small, steady steps forward.

July 9th

Steadfast in Life's Chaos

SCRIPTURE
"Let us not become weary in doing good, for at the proper time we will reap a harvest if we do not give up." - Galatians 6:9

REFLECTION
Amid life's unpredictable moments—sick children, work demands, or unexpected challenges—maintaining consistent practices anchors our days in peace. Rather than seeking perfection, focus on returning to your core habits with grace. When disruptions come, adjust your approach while keeping your commitment to what matters most.

PRAYER
Faithful Father, strengthen me to maintain steady practices even when life feels chaotic. Help me adapt with flexibility while staying true to my core commitments. Thank You for Your constant presence that guides me through every season. Grant me wisdom to adjust without abandoning what matters most. Amen.

POSITIVE THOUGHT OF THE DAY
I remain steady in my commitments through life's changing seasons.

July 10th

Shaping Your Vision of Success

SCRIPTURE
"For we are his handiwork, created in Christ Jesus for the good works that God has prepared in advance." - Ephesians 2:10

REFLECTION
Creating a clear picture of success in your mind isn't about perfection—it's about possibility. Take time today to envision what peace, balance, and joy look like in your unique situation. Whether it's maintaining calm during morning routines or finding time for prayer, let this vision guide your steps forward. Remember that God has already prepared good works for you to accomplish.

PRAYER
Creator God, help me see the possibilities You've placed before me. Guide my thoughts toward Your vision for my life. Thank You for creating me with purpose and potential. Grant me clarity to recognize and pursue the path You've prepared. Amen.

POSITIVE THOUGHT OF THE DAY
I see clearly the path God has prepared for me.

July 11th

Transforming Negative Thoughts

SCRIPTURE
"Finally, brothers, whatever is true, whatever is honorable, whatever is just, whatever is pure, whatever is lovely, whatever is gracious, if there is any excellence and if there is anything worthy of praise, think about these things." - Philippians 4:8

REFLECTION
Your thoughts shape your reality. When self-doubt whispers "I'm not good enough," counter it with truth: "I am growing and learning each day." Replace "I'll never manage this" with "I can take small steps forward." These shifts in thinking aren't just positive thinking—they're aligning your mind with God's truth about your worth and capability.

PRAYER
Lord of Truth, guide my thoughts toward what uplifts and strengthens. Help me recognize negative patterns and replace them with Your truth. Thank You for showing me my worth through Your eyes. Lead me to thoughts that build rather than break down. Amen.

POSITIVE THOUGHT OF THE DAY
I choose thoughts that align with God's truth about me.

July 12th

Standing in Your Authentic Self

SCRIPTURE
"Before I formed you in the womb I knew you, before you were born I dedicated you." - Jeremiah 1:5

REFLECTION
True confidence blooms when you honor your authentic self rather than copying others. Your unique way of mothering, working, and living is a gift. Instead of comparing yourself to other mothers or trying to mirror their methods, recognize that God designed you with specific strengths and gifts for your particular journey.

PRAYER
Loving Father, thank You for creating me uniquely. Help me recognize and value my authentic gifts and ways of being. Free me from the need to copy others or seek their approval. Grant me confidence in the person You created me to be. Amen.

POSITIVE THOUGHT OF THE DAY
I trust in the unique way God created me to mother and live.

July 13th

Finding Joy in God's Rhythm

SCRIPTURE
"Rejoice in the Lord always. I shall say it again: rejoice!" - Philippians 4:4

REFLECTION
True happiness flows from aligning our daily lives with God's divine rhythm. Today, notice the moments where you can transform routine tasks into sacred offerings—whether saying grace before meals, sharing faith discussions with your children, or finding quiet moments for prayer. These aren't just activities to check off, but opportunities to sync your heart with God's tempo for your life.

PRAYER
Lord of Joy, help me recognize Your rhythm in my daily life. Guide me to transform ordinary moments into occasions of grace. Thank You for showing me that true happiness comes from living in harmony with Your design. Lead me to choose joy in all circumstances. Amen.

POSITIVE THOUGHT OF THE DAY
I discover joy by flowing with God's divine rhythm.

July 14th

Sacred Moments in Nature

SCRIPTURE
"The heavens declare the glory of God; the skies proclaim the work of his hands." - Psalm 19:1

REFLECTION
God's presence surrounds us in creation—from morning birdsong to evening sunset. When we pause to notice these natural rhythms, we align ourselves with His divine design. Today, take time to experience God's presence in nature, whether through a walk in the park, sitting on your porch, or simply watching clouds drift by. These moments of connection restore our spirits and remind us of His constant presence.

PRAYER
Creator God, open my eyes to Your presence in nature's beauty. Help me find moments to pause and connect with Your creation. Thank You for revealing Your glory in the world around me. Renew my spirit through these sacred encounters with Your handiwork. Amen.

POSITIVE THOUGHT OF THE DAY
I find peace and joy in nature's sacred rhythms.

July 15th

Service With a Joyful Heart

SCRIPTURE
"Give and gifts will be given to you; a good measure, packed together, shaken down, and overflowing, will be poured into your lap." - Luke 6:38

REFLECTION
Joy multiplies when we serve others with love. Transform your daily tasks from obligations into opportunities for giving—whether folding laundry, preparing meals, or caring for your family. Each act of service, done with conscious love, aligns us with God's generous heart and fills us with authentic happiness. Remember that these seemingly mundane moments can become channels of grace when offered with love.

PRAYER
Generous Father, help me see each task as an opportunity to serve with love. Transform my perspective on daily duties from burden to blessing. Thank You for the joy that comes through giving. Guide me to find happiness in serving others as You serve us. Amen.

POSITIVE THOUGHT OF THE DAY
I find joy in serving others with a loving heart.

July 16th

Setting Sacred Boundaries

SCRIPTURE
"But let your 'Yes' mean 'Yes,' and your 'No' mean 'No.' Anything more is from the evil one." - Matthew 5:37

REFLECTION
When we overextend ourselves, we often diminish our capacity to serve with joy and purpose. Today, examine your commitments: Are they aligned with your core values and current season of life? Remember that saying 'no' to excess creates space to say 'yes' to what truly matters. Your worth isn't measured by how many tasks you accomplish, but by your identity as God's beloved child.

PRAYER
Wise Father, grant me discernment to recognize my limits and courage to honor them. Help me choose commitments that align with Your will for my life. Thank You for loving me beyond my accomplishments. Guide me to find peace in living within Your designed boundaries. Amen.

POSITIVE THOUGHT OF THE DAY
I honor my limits as holy boundaries set with love.

July 17th

Beyond the Badge of Busyness

SCRIPTURE
"Come to me, all you who labor and are burdened, and I will give you rest." - Matthew 11:28

REFLECTION
Busyness isn't a measure of worth or success. When we treat exhaustion as a badge of honor, we miss the sacred rhythms God designed for our lives. Consider how overcommitment affects your spiritual, physical, and emotional wellbeing. True productivity flows not from endless activity, but from purposeful choices that leave room for rest and renewal.

PRAYER
Lord of Rest, free me from the need to prove my worth through constant activity. Help me recognize when I'm operating from depletion rather than devotion. Thank You for offering true rest in Your presence. Guide me to a pace that honors both service and stillness. Amen.

POSITIVE THOUGHT OF THE DAY
I choose purposeful action over endless activity.

July 18th

Rooted in True Worth

SCRIPTURE
"You formed my inmost being; you knit me in my mother's womb. I praise you, because I am wonderfully made." - Psalm 139:13-14

REFLECTION
Our value doesn't stem from what we do, but from who we are—beloved children of God. When we tie our worth to productivity, we create an endless cycle of striving that leads to burnout. Today, pause to remember that your dignity comes from being created in God's image, not from your accomplishments or others' approval.

PRAYER
Creator God, help me remember that my worth comes from You alone. Release me from the need to prove myself through endless doing. Thank You for loving me completely, exactly as I am. Ground me in the truth of my identity as Your cherished child. Amen.

POSITIVE THOUGHT OF THE DAY
My worth flows from God's love, not my achievements.

July 19th

Finding Joy in Small Moments

SCRIPTURE
"Rejoice always, pray without ceasing, give thanks in all circumstances; for this is the will of God in Christ Jesus for you." - 1 Thessalonians 5:16-18

REFLECTION
Like a dull gem transformed through polishing, ordinary moments can shine with unexpected beauty when viewed with mindful attention. Today, notice the small gifts in your daily routines—a child's laughter, morning sunlight, the aroma of coffee. These aren't mere distractions from life's challenges but rather divine invitations to experience God's presence in the ordinary.

PRAYER
Gracious Lord, open my eyes to the hidden treasures in everyday moments. Help me notice Your presence in the simple gifts that surround me. Thank You for the countless ways You reveal Your love throughout my day. Guide me to find delight in what I might normally overlook. Amen.

POSITIVE THOUGHT OF THE DAY
I discover God's gifts in life's simple moments.

July 20th

Rekindling Sacred Passions

SCRIPTURE
"Delight yourself in the Lord, and he will give you the desires of your heart." - Psalm 37:4

REFLECTION
Each soul carries unique interests and passions planted by God. When life feels mundane, reconnecting with these God-given desires can restore our sense of purpose. Whether through creative pursuits, time in nature, or moments of quiet reflection, pursuing these passions isn't selfish—it's honoring the unique way God made you to experience and share His joy.

PRAYER
Creator God, help me rediscover the passions You've placed in my heart. Guide me to make space for activities that bring wholesome joy. Thank You for designing me with unique interests and abilities. Show me how to use these gifts to bring delight to myself and others. Amen.

POSITIVE THOUGHT OF THE DAY
I honor God by pursuing the passions He placed within me.

July 21st

Transforming Tasks Through Gratitude

SCRIPTURE
"I will give thanks to you, Lord, with all my heart; I will tell of all your wonderful deeds." - Psalm 9:1

REFLECTION
Like sunflowers turning toward light, gratitude can reorient our perspective on daily tasks. Even routine responsibilities can become opportunities for thanksgiving—having a home to clean, family to cook for, work to do. When we view our tasks through the lens of gratitude, what once felt like drudgery can transform into moments of grace.

PRAYER
Lord of Light, help me see my daily tasks through eyes of gratitude. Transform my perspective from obligation to opportunity. Thank You for the countless blessings disguised as routine responsibilities. Guide me to find joy in serving through everyday moments. Amen.

POSITIVE THOUGHT OF THE DAY
Gratitude transforms my tasks into opportunities for joy.

July 22nd

Finding Sacred Balance

SCRIPTURE
"Come to me, all you who labor and are burdened, and I will give you rest." - Matthew 11:28

REFLECTION
God designed us with rhythms of productivity and rest—both are sacred gifts. Like the natural cycles of day and night, our bodies and spirits need times of focused energy and quiet renewal. Instead of measuring your worth by what you accomplish, recognize that both your doing and your being reflect God's image. Today, notice which rhythm your body and spirit are calling for.

PRAYER
Wise Creator, help me honor the rhythms You've designed for my life. Guide me to recognize when to be productive and when to rest. Thank You for showing me that both activity and stillness are sacred. Grant me wisdom to flow between these states with grace. Amen.

POSITIVE THOUGHT OF THE DAY
I honor both my productivity and rest as sacred gifts fro

July 23rd

Rest Without Guilt

SCRIPTURE
"In peace I will lie down and fall asleep, for you alone, LORD, make me secure." - Psalm 4:9

REFLECTION
Rest isn't laziness—it's holy restoration. When we resist taking breaks, we work against our God-given design for renewal. Consider how Jesus often withdrew to quiet places despite endless needs around Him. Your worth isn't measured by constant activity but by your identity as God's beloved child. Let this truth free you to receive the gift of rest without guilt.

PRAYER
Lord of Rest, free me from guilt when I pause to restore my spirit. Help me trust that taking time to rest serves both my family and You. Thank You for modeling the importance of renewal through Jesus' example. Grant me peace in moments of stillness. Amen.

POSITIVE THOUGHT OF THE DAY
I receive rest as a gift that renews my spirit and serves my family.

July 24th

Working from Grace

SCRIPTURE
"For we are his handiwork, created in Christ Jesus for good works that God has prepared in advance." - Ephesians 2:10

REFLECTION
Productivity flows best from a place of grace, not striving. When we remember our worth comes from being God's children, not our achievements, we can work from a place of freedom rather than pressure. Today, notice if you're pushing yourself from obligation or moving from love. Let your actions flow from knowing you're already enough in God's eyes.

PRAYER
Gracious Father, help me work from a place of love rather than pressure to prove my worth. Guide me to serve from the security of being Your beloved child. Thank You for loving me completely apart from my accomplishments. Let this truth free me to work with joy. Amen.

POSITIVE THOUGHT OF THE DAY
I work from grace, knowing I am already enough in God's eyes.

July 25th

Finding Worth Beyond Comparison

SCRIPTURE
"We are God's handiwork, created in Christ Jesus to do good works, which God prepared in advance for us to do." - Ephesians 2:10

REFLECTION
When we constantly measure ourselves against others, we miss the unique beauty God crafted in us. Like different flowers in a garden, each mother has her own gifts and timing for blooming. Today, notice when comparison thoughts arise and gently redirect your focus to the specific ways God equipped you for your unique journey of motherhood.

PRAYER
Creator God, help me recognize and cherish the unique way You've designed me. When comparison tempts me, guide my thoughts back to Your perfect plan for my life. Thank You for making me exactly as I am. Grant me eyes to see my worth through Your loving gaze. Amen.

POSITIVE THOUGHT OF THE DAY
I honor my unique path as God's beloved creation.

July 26th

Moving from Comparison to Compassion

SCRIPTURE
"Let us not become conceited, provoking one another, envying one another." - Galatians 5:26

REFLECTION
Behind every seemingly perfect life lies hidden struggles and challenges. Rather than comparing our weaknesses to others' perceived strengths, we can choose compassion—both for ourselves and others. When you notice comparison arising, remember that each mother faces her own unique journey of joys and difficulties. This understanding frees us to celebrate others while honoring our own path.

PRAYER
Merciful Father, transform my tendency to compare into compassion for myself and others. Help me remember that every family's journey is unique. Thank You for teaching me to see beyond surface appearances. Guide me to encourage rather than compare. Amen.

POSITIVE THOUGHT OF THE DAY
I choose compassion over comparison, celebrating each unique journey.

July 27th

Growing in Gratitude

SCRIPTURE
"I praise you because I am fearfully and wonderfully made; your works are wonderful, I know that full well." - Psalm 139:14

REFLECTION
Gratitude is the antidote to comparison. When we focus on our blessings—our children's unique personalities, our family's special traditions, our own growing wisdom as mothers—comparison loses its power. Today, instead of noticing what others have that you don't, count the specific gifts God has woven into your life and family.

PRAYER
Gracious God, open my eyes to the countless blessings You've placed in my life. When comparison tempts me, help me pivot to gratitude. Thank You for the unique gifts You've given my family. Let appreciation fill my heart and guide my thoughts. Amen.

POSITIVE THOUGHT OF THE DAY
Gratitude fills my heart, leaving no room for comparison.

July 28th

Sacred Self-Investment

SCRIPTURE
"Do you not know that your body is a temple of the Holy Spirit within you, whom you have from God?" - 1 Corinthians 6:19

REFLECTION
Just as we nurture our children's growth, God invites us to tend to our own development. When we invest in our wellbeing—whether through learning, rest, or renewal—we honor the temple God created. Today, notice where you might be withholding permission from yourself to grow, learn, or simply be. Remember that caring for yourself is not selfish but sacred.

PRAYER
Generous God, help me recognize that investing in myself honors Your creation. Release me from guilt when I take time to grow and renew. Thank You for entrusting me with this temple of body, mind, and spirit. Guide me to care for myself as lovingly as You care for me. Amen.

POSITIVE THOUGHT OF THE DAY
I honor God by investing in my growth and wellbeing.

July 29th

Embracing Holy Imperfection

SCRIPTURE
"But he said to me, 'My grace is sufficient for you, for my power is made perfect in weakness.'" - 2 Corinthians 12:9

REFLECTION
Perfection belongs to God alone; our humanity includes beautiful imperfection. When we give ourselves permission to be wrong, to make mistakes, to learn and grow, we open ourselves to God's grace. These moments of weakness become opportunities for God's strength to shine through. Today, practice extending to yourself the same grace God so freely gives.

PRAYER
Merciful Father, help me accept my human limitations with grace. When I stumble, remind me that Your love doesn't depend on my perfection. Thank You for loving me completely, even in my mistakes. Grant me courage to embrace my humanity fully. Amen.

POSITIVE THOUGHT OF THE DAY
I receive God's grace in my imperfections and growth.

July 30th

Setting Sacred Boundaries

SCRIPTURE
"Above all else, guard your heart, for everything you do flows from it." - Proverbs 4:23

REFLECTION
Setting boundaries isn't just about saying no—it's about creating sacred space to say yes to what truly matters. Like Jesus who often withdrew to quiet places despite endless needs around Him, we too must protect our time and energy for what God calls us to do. Remember that boundaries aren't barriers but holy limits that help us serve from abundance rather than depletion.

PRAYER
Lord of Wisdom, grant me discernment to set healthy boundaries in my life. Help me recognize when to say yes and when to say no. Thank You for showing me that limits can be loving. Guide me to protect the sacred space You've given me to nurture. Amen.

POSITIVE THOUGHT OF THE DAY
My boundaries create space for God's best in my life.

July 31st

Loving Our Whole Selves

SCRIPTURE
"I praise you because I am fearfully and wonderfully made; your works are wonderful, I know that full well." - Psalm 139:14

REFLECTION
God's love for us is complete and unconditional—embracing our strengths, weaknesses, successes, and struggles. When we give ourselves permission to love all aspects of who we are, we reflect God's total acceptance of us. Like a masterpiece that includes both light and shadow, our whole selves—including what we perceive as flaws—were purposefully crafted by our Creator. Today, practice extending love to every part of yourself, knowing that God designed each aspect with purpose.

PRAYER
Loving Creator, help me embrace all aspects of who You made me to be. When I struggle to accept parts of myself, remind me of Your complete and unconditional love. Thank You for creating me with purpose, even in what I perceive as weaknesses. Guide me to love myself as fully as You love me. Amen.

POSITIVE THOUGHT OF THE DAY
I honor God by loving all of who He created me to be.

August

August 1st

Living with Sacred Purpose

SCRIPTURE
"For I know well the plans I have in mind for you, says the LORD, plans for your welfare and not for woe, so as to give you a future of hope." - Jeremiah 29:11

REFLECTION
Just as a compass guides a traveler, a clear sense of mission guides our daily choices. Today, consider what truly matters in your current season of life. What values and priorities has God placed on your heart? When we align our actions with our deepest values, even ordinary tasks become meaningful expressions of our purpose. Let your decisions flow from this clarity of mission.

PRAYER
Divine Guide, help me recognize the unique purpose You've given me in this season. Grant me wisdom to align my choices with what matters most. Thank You for showing me that even simple tasks can reflect Your glory when done with purpose. Guide my steps according to Your perfect plan. Amen.

POSITIVE THOUGHT OF THE DAY
I live with purpose, letting my values guide each choice.

August 2nd

Crafting Life's Sacred Direction

SCRIPTURE
"Teach us to count our days aright, that we may gain wisdom of heart." - Psalm 90:12

REFLECTION
God gives each season of motherhood its own sacred calling. Rather than spreading ourselves thin trying to do everything, we can focus on what matters most right now. Take time today to define your current mission—whether it's creating a faith-filled home, nurturing young hearts, or guiding older children. Let this clarity become your anchor in daily decisions.

PRAYER
Lord of Wisdom, help me discern my unique mission in this season of motherhood. Give me courage to focus on what truly matters now. Thank

You for showing me that different seasons require different priorities. Grant me peace in living according to Your purpose for this time. Amen.

POSITIVE THOUGHT OF THE DAY
I embrace my sacred mission in this season of life.

August 3rd

Walking in Faith's Direction

SCRIPTURE
"Your word is a lamp for my feet, a light for my path." - Psalm 119:105

REFLECTION
When we have a clear mission, decisions become simpler—not always easier, but clearer. Like a lamp illuminating our path, our mission statement helps us see which opportunities to embrace and which to release. Today, let your values and purpose guide your choices, trusting that saying no to good things allows you to say yes to God's best for this season.

PRAYER
Faithful Father, illuminate my path through the mission You've given me. When decisions arise, help me choose based on the purpose You've placed in my heart. Thank You for providing clear direction through my values and priorities. Keep me focused on Your perfect plan. Amen.

POSITIVE THOUGHT OF THE DAY
My mission guides me toward God's best for my life.

August 4th

Healing Through Forgiveness

SCRIPTURE
"Bear with one another and, if anyone has a complaint against another, forgive each other; just as the Lord has forgiven you, so you also must forgive." - Colossians 3:13

REFLECTION
Just as we treat physical wounds promptly to prevent infection, our spiritual wounds need immediate care through forgiveness. When others hurt us, our first response can be to hold tight to the injury, replaying it in our minds. Yet God invites us to a different path—applying the healing balm of forgiveness, not just for others but for our own peace. Today, notice where you're holding onto hurt and ask God for the grace to begin healing.

PRAYER
Merciful Father, help me release the hurts I carry before they become deep wounds of resentment. Teach me to apply Your healing forgiveness quickly when others wound me. Thank You for showing me that forgiveness brings freedom. Grant me strength to let go and heal. Amen.

POSITIVE THOUGHT OF THE DAY
I choose healing over holding onto hurt.

August 5th

Seeking God's Perspective

SCRIPTURE
"Be kind to one another, tenderhearted, forgiving one another, as God in Christ has forgiven you." - Ephesians 4:32

REFLECTION
When others wound us, seeking God's perspective can transform our response. Remember that every person—even those who hurt us—is God's beloved child, often acting from their own pain or struggles. This understanding doesn't excuse hurtful actions but helps us respond with compassion rather than resentment. Today, practice seeing difficult people through God's eyes of love.

PRAYER
Lord of Understanding, help me see others as You see them, especially when they hurt me. Guide me to respond with compassion rather than resentment. Thank You for loving all Your children, even in our brokenness. Grant me Your perspective in challenging relationships. Amen.

POSITIVE THOUGHT OF THE DAY
I view others through God's lens of love and understanding.

August 6th

Freedom in Letting Go

SCRIPTURE
"Let all bitterness and wrath and anger and clamor and slander be put away from you, along with all malice." - Ephesians 4:31

REFLECTION
Holding onto resentment is like carrying a heavy burden that only weighs us down. True freedom comes not in waiting for others to make amends, but in choosing to release our grip on past hurts. This doesn't mean forgetting or excusing harmful actions, but rather choosing our own

peace over nursing wounds. Today, identify where you can lay down the weight of resentment.

PRAYER
God of Peace, help me release the burdens of resentment I carry. When others hurt me, guide me to choose freedom through forgiveness. Thank You for showing me that letting go brings healing. Grant me courage to release past hurts into Your care. Amen.

POSITIVE THOUGHT OF THE DAY
I find freedom in releasing resentment to God.

August 7th

Sacred Time With God

SCRIPTURE
"Be still, and know that I am God." - Psalm 46:10

REFLECTION
Just as children thrive on quality time with their parents, our spirits flourish when we dedicate time to be with our Heavenly Father. This isn't about perfecting prayers or following strict routines—it's about creating space in our busy lives for divine connection. Today, consider how you might carve out moments for sacred communion, whether through quiet prayer, meditation on Scripture, or simply sitting in God's presence.

PRAYER
Lord of Peace, help me prioritize time with You amid life's busyness. Show me how to create spaces of stillness where I can hear Your voice. Thank You for always being present, waiting to commune with me. Guide me to make our time together sacred and regular. Amen.

POSITIVE THOUGHT OF THE DAY
I grow closer to God's design through dedicated time with Him.

August 8th

Opening to Divine Grace

SCRIPTURE
"Draw near to God, and he will draw near to you." - James 4:8

REFLECTION
Like flowers opening to sunlight, our souls unfold in God's presence. When we regularly set aside time for prayer and communion with God, we position ourselves to receive His countless blessings and guidance.

These sacred moments aren't just religious duties but opportunities for transformation—chances to become more fully who God created us to be.

PRAYER
Loving Father, help me create regular times to sit in Your presence. Open my heart to receive Your grace during these moments. Thank You for the gift of communion with You. Let these times transform me into who You designed me to be. Amen.

POSITIVE THOUGHT OF THE DAY
I open myself to God's transforming presence each day.

August 9th

Guided by The Spirit

SCRIPTURE
"When the Spirit of truth comes, he will guide you into all the truth." - John 16:13

REFLECTION
Regular communion with God creates space for the Holy Spirit to order our thoughts and guide our steps. Like clearing a path through overgrown brush, dedicated prayer time helps remove the clutter of worldly concerns, allowing divine wisdom to flow more freely in our lives. These moments of connection become foundations for living out God's design for us.

PRAYER
Holy Spirit, guide my thoughts and actions through our times of communion. Clear away whatever blocks me from hearing Your voice clearly. Thank You for Your constant presence and guidance. Help me prioritize our time together so I can better follow Your lead. Amen.

POSITIVE THOUGHT OF THE DAY
The Holy Spirit guides me as I make time for God.

August 10th

Sacred Rest for the Soul

SCRIPTURE
"He makes me lie down in green pastures, he leads me beside quiet waters, he refreshes my soul." - Psalm 23:2-3

REFLECTION

Unlike machines that run continuously, God designed us with a need for rest and renewal. This isn't weakness—it's wisdom built into our very nature. When we resist this design by pushing ourselves endlessly, we work against God's rhythm for our lives. Today, honor your need for rest as a holy gift, recognizing that pausing to refresh your soul makes you more, not less, effective in serving others.

PRAYER
Gentle Shepherd, help me honor the rhythms of rest You've woven into my design. Release me from guilt when I need to pause and renew. Thank You for modeling sacred rest through Your creation. Guide me to find peace in moments of stillness. Amen.

POSITIVE THOUGHT OF THE DAY
I honor God's design by embracing my need for rest.

August 11th

Divine Rhythms of Renewal

SCRIPTURE
"Come away by yourselves to a deserted place and rest a while." - Mark 6:31

REFLECTION
Just as Jesus called His disciples aside for rest, He invites us to step away from constant doing to simply be. These aren't moments of laziness but sacred pauses that restore our spirits and realign our hearts with God's purpose. Whether through quiet prayer, gentle movement, or peaceful solitude, making space for renewal honors our humanity and strengthens our ability to serve with love.

PRAYER
Lord of Rest, help me recognize when I need to step away and renew my spirit. Give me courage to honor these sacred pauses without guilt. Thank You for showing me that rest strengthens rather than weakens my service. Guide me in finding regular moments of renewal. Amen.

POSITIVE THOUGHT OF THE DAY
I find strength in sacred moments of renewal.

August 12th

Embracing Our Human Design

SCRIPTURE
"Even youths grow tired and weary, and young men stumble and fall; but those who hope in the LORD will renew their strength." - Isaiah 40:30-31

REFLECTION
Accepting our human limitations isn't defeat—it's wisdom. Unlike machines, we were created to flourish through cycles of activity and rest, work and renewal. When we acknowledge our need for replenishment, we align with God's perfect design for our lives. Today, notice where you're pushing beyond your limits and choose instead to honor your God-given need for renewal.

PRAYER
Creator God, thank You for designing me with wisdom, including my need for rest. Help me remember that my limitations are not flaws but invitations to depend on You. Guide me to balance activity with renewal, trusting Your perfect plan for my wellbeing. Amen.

POSITIVE THOUGHT OF THE DAY
My need for renewal reflects God's perfect design.

August 13th

Living in Divine Truth

SCRIPTURE
"You will know the truth, and the truth will set you free." - John 8:32

REFLECTION
Our minds often whisper lies that diminish our worth—that we're not enough, that our daily work lacks meaning, that our gifts are insignificant. Yet God's truth speaks differently. Every talent, every act of motherly care, every moment spent nurturing your family holds eternal value. Today, notice when these lies surface and counter them with God's truth about your worth.

PRAYER
Lord of Truth, help me recognize and reject the lies that diminish my worth. Guide me to see myself through Your eyes of love. Thank You for the unique gifts You've given me. Grant me wisdom to live in Your truth rather than the world's lies. Amen.

POSITIVE THOUGHT OF THE DAY
I choose to live in God's truth about my worth.

August 14th

Treasured as God's Creation

SCRIPTURE
"I give praise to you, for I am fearfully and wonderfully made." - Psalm 139:14

REFLECTION
God doesn't create anything ordinary or insignificant. Your unique blend of talents, personality, and maternal instincts were purposefully crafted. When thoughts of inadequacy arise, remember that the Master Creator designed you specifically for your family and purpose. Your daily acts of love—even the smallest ones—reflect His creative wisdom.

PRAYER
Creator God, help me see the beauty and purpose You've woven into my being. When I doubt my worth, remind me of Your perfect design. Thank You for creating me uniquely for my family and purpose. Let me reflect Your love in all I do. Amen.

POSITIVE THOUGHT OF THE DAY
I honor God's design by embracing my unique gifts.

August 15th

Finding Peace in Present Grace

SCRIPTURE
"My grace is sufficient for you, for power is made perfect in weakness." - 2 Corinthians 12:9

REFLECTION
The lie that we must "finish everything" before finding peace keeps us from experiencing God's present grace. Peace isn't waiting at some future finish line—it's available now, even amid unfolded laundry and unchecked tasks. Today, choose to find joy in the journey rather than postponing it until everything is "perfect."

PRAYER
Gracious Father, help me find peace in Your presence rather than in completed tasks. Show me how to enjoy life's journey instead of always rushing to the next goal. Thank You for offering grace for this moment. Guide me to receive Your peace right where I am. Amen.

POSITIVE THOUGHT OF THE DAY
I embrace God's grace in this present moment.

August 16th

Finding Purpose in Quiet Seasons

SCRIPTURE
"To everything there is a season, and a time for every purpose under heaven." - Ecclesiastes 3:1

REFLECTION
Just as nature moves through seasons of vibrancy and rest, our spirits experience times of energy and stillness. When life feels monotonous, remember these moments offer space for deeper connection with God. Rather than resist these quieter seasons, we can welcome them as opportunities to listen more closely to God's whispers, reflect on our path, and gather strength for times of growth ahead.

PRAYER
Lord of Every Season, help me recognize Your purpose in times that feel ordinary. When life seems colorless, open my eyes to the gifts hidden in stillness. Thank You for these moments to pause and realign my heart with Yours. Guide me to find meaning in every season You provide. Amen.

POSITIVE THOUGHT OF THE DAY
I discover God's purpose in every season of life.

August 17th

Growing Through Stillness

SCRIPTURE
"In returning and rest you shall be saved; in quietness and in trust shall be your strength." - Isaiah 30:15

REFLECTION
When days feel mundane, they invite us to discover joy in simple moments—a child's laughter, morning sunlight, shared meals. These ordinary times aren't empty spaces but fertile ground where God cultivates deeper faith. Today, notice the small gifts tucked within routine moments, knowing God works even in seasons that feel unremarkable.

PRAYER
Patient Father, help me appreciate the quiet moments You provide. When life feels routine, show me the beauty in ordinary days. Thank You for working in every season of my journey. Lead me to find refreshment in times of stillness. Amen.

POSITIVE THOUGHT OF THE DAY
I find hidden treasures in ordinary moments.

August 18th

Moving Beyond Monotony

SCRIPTURE
"The Lord will guide you always; he will satisfy your needs in a sun-scorched land." - Isaiah 58:11

REFLECTION
Rather than viewing monotonous days as obstacles, we can receive them as invitations—to try something new, reach out to others, or deepen our prayer life. When routines feel stale, God often uses these moments to nudge us toward growth. Consider what fresh path He might be preparing, what new connection He might be orchestrating through this slower season.

PRAYER
Divine Guide, reveal fresh possibilities in familiar routines. When life feels colorless, inspire me with Your creative Spirit. Thank You for using every season to shape my journey. Help me step forward in faith when You call me to new paths. Amen.

POSITIVE THOUGHT OF THE DAY
I discover new paths when I follow God's lead.

August 19th

Choosing with Confidence

SCRIPTURE
"Trust in the LORD with all your heart and lean not on your own understanding." - Proverbs 3:5

REFLECTION
When decisions paralyze us with fear of missing out, God invites us to shift our focus from what we might lose to what He provides. Rather than comparing our path to others', we can turn inward to examine our values and current season. Today, notice if comparison is freezing your choices and ask God to illuminate what truly matters for your family in this moment.

PRAYER
Wise Father, guide my decisions with Your wisdom. When choices overwhelm me, help me focus on Your priorities for my life. Thank You for leading me with love. Grant me peace to trust the path You've marked. Amen.

POSITIVE THOUGHT OF THE DAY
I choose confidently, guided by God's wisdom.

August 20th

Present in His Plan

SCRIPTURE
"For I know well the plans I have in mind for you, says the LORD, plans for your welfare and not for woe." - Jeremiah 29:11

REFLECTION
God's plan unfolds in our present moment, not in endless "what-ifs" about paths not taken. When we constantly look over our shoulder at others' journeys, we miss the gifts He's placed in our own. Today, rather than questioning your choices, notice the specific ways God is working in your current circumstances.

PRAYER
Lord of Every Moment, help me recognize Your presence in my daily path. When I'm tempted to question my choices, remind me of Your faithful guidance. Thank You for Your perfect plan for my life. Keep my heart anchored in today's blessings. Amen.

POSITIVE THOUGHT OF THE DAY
I trust God's plan unfolding in my present path.

August 21st

Walking Forward in Faith

SCRIPTURE
"Your word is a lamp for my feet, a light for my path." - Psalm 119:105

REFLECTION
Faith moves forward one step at a time, not paralyzed by endless options but trusting God's guidance for each choice. Like a lamp that illuminates just the next step, God provides wisdom for today's decisions. We don't need to see the entire path—just enough light for our next faithful choice.

PRAYER
Faithful Guide, strengthen me to move forward with confidence in Your direction. When choices overwhelm me, light my next step. Thank You for Your constant guidance. Help me trust Your leading even when I can't see the full path. Amen.

POSITIVE THOUGHT OF THE DAY
I take each step forward with faith in God's guidance.

August 22nd

Building Peace Through Small Steps

SCRIPTURE
"He who is faithful in a very little is faithful also in much." - Luke 16:10

REFLECTION
Like water shaping stone drop by drop, small daily actions create lasting change in our spiritual lives. When we dedicate even a few minutes each day to nurturing our connection with God, these moments compound into profound peace. Rather than seeking dramatic transformations, focus on consistent, minor adjustments in your daily routine—a brief morning prayer, a moment of gratitude, or a few minutes of spiritual reading. These seemingly modest practices, when done faithfully, shape the foundation of lasting peace.

PRAYER
Loving Father, help me value the power of small, faithful actions in my journey toward peace. Guide me to maintain consistency in these daily practices that draw me closer to You. Thank You for showing me that transformation comes through steady dedication. Grant me the wisdom to trust in the compounding effect of these modest steps. Amen.

POSITIVE THOUGHT OF THE DAY
I build lasting peace through small, faithful daily actions.

August 23rd

Cultivating Inner Calm

SCRIPTURE
"You will keep in perfect peace those whose minds are steadfast, because they trust in you." - Isaiah 26:3

REFLECTION
Our daily choices shape our experience of peace. Each moment offers an opportunity to choose thoughts that foster calm over chaos. Remember that peace isn't found in perfecting circumstances but in aligning our minds with God's truth. Today, practice noticing your thought patterns and gently redirecting them toward peace-building perspectives. Small shifts in how you view challenges can compound into profound inner tranquility over time.

PRAYER
Divine Guide, help me choose thoughts that cultivate peace in my heart. When chaos surrounds me, steady my mind on Your unchanging truth.

Thank You for the power to shape my inner world through my choices.
Lead me toward patterns of thinking that build lasting serenity. Amen.

POSITIVE THOUGHT OF THE DAY
I choose thoughts that compound into deep, lasting peace.

August 24th

Priorities and Peace

SCRIPTURE
"Seek first his kingdom and his righteousness, and all these things will be
given to you as well." - Matthew 6:33

REFLECTION
Peace multiplies when we align our priorities with God's wisdom. Each day
brings countless demands, but true serenity grows as we learn to put our
relationship with God first. This spiritual foundation helps us discern what
truly matters in our daily choices. When we dedicate even brief moments
to nurturing our connection with God, these small investments compound
into a deeper, more sustainable peace that guides all other decisions.

PRAYER
Lord of Wisdom, guide me in ordering my priorities according to Your
will. Help me see that small moments spent with You multiply into lasting
peace. Thank You for showing me that everything falls into place when
You are first in my life. Grant me clarity to maintain this divine order in
my daily choices. Amen.

POSITIVE THOUGHT OF THE DAY
My peace grows when I align my priorities with God's wisdom.

August 25th

Freedom from Perfection

SCRIPTURE
"But he said to me, 'My grace is sufficient for you, for power is made
perfect in weakness.'" - 2 Corinthians 12:9

REFLECTION
Our worth isn't measured by flawless performance but by our identity as
God's beloved children. When we release the need for perfection—in our
homes, our parenting, our appearance—we open ourselves to experience
true joy. Today, notice where perfectionism holds you back from taking
action or experiencing peace. Remember that God's grace fills the gaps

in our human limitations. Choose progress over perfection, knowing that small steps forward, even imperfect ones, lead to growth.

PRAYER
Merciful Father, help me release the burden of perfectionism. Guide me to accept Your grace in my weaknesses and limitations. Thank You for loving me completely, exactly as I am. Grant me wisdom to choose progress over perfection, trusting in Your sufficiency rather than my own strength. Amen.

POSITIVE THOUGHT OF THE DAY
I find freedom in choosing progress over perfection.

August 26th

Living Your Authentic Path

SCRIPTURE
"For we are his handiwork, created in Christ Jesus for good works, which God prepared in advance." - Ephesians 2:10

REFLECTION
Comparing ourselves to others dims the unique light God placed within us. Each family's journey holds its own timing, challenges, and victories. When we focus on others' paths, we miss the beauty of our own. Today, practice turning comparison into gratitude—thanking God for your unique gifts, your family's special moments, and the specific ways He's equipped you for your journey. Your worth isn't measured against others but found in being exactly who God created you to be.

PRAYER
Creator God, help me appreciate the unique path You've set before me. When comparison tempts me, turn my heart toward gratitude. Thank You for designing me with purpose and intention. Guide me to celebrate my journey without measuring it against others. Amen.

POSITIVE THOUGHT OF THE DAY
I honor my unique path as God's cherished creation.

August 27th

Finding Peace in Stillness

SCRIPTURE
"Be still, and know that I am God." - Psalm 46:10

REFLECTION
Busyness isn't a badge of honor—it's often a barrier to peace. When we measure our worth by our activity level, we miss opportunities for deeper

connection with God and our loved ones. Today, challenge the belief that constant motion equals importance. Create moments of intentional stillness in your day. These pauses aren't wasted time but vital spaces where God can speak to your heart and restore your spirit.

PRAYER
Lord of Peace, help me value stillness as much as activity. When busyness tempts me, remind me that my worth isn't measured by my productivity. Thank You for meeting me in quiet moments. Guide me to create space for stillness in my daily life. Amen.

POSITIVE THOUGHT OF THE DAY
I find strength and purpose in moments of stillness with God.

August 28th

Moving Forward Step by Step

SCRIPTURE
"Your word is a lamp for my feet, a light on my path." - Psalm 119:105

REFLECTION
Just as a bridge spans challenging waters, God provides ways to move from negative thoughts to positive ones. Today, rather than expecting instant transformation, look for small steps forward in your thinking. When you catch yourself in patterns of negativity, pause and ask: "What's one thought that feels a little better?" Remember, progress doesn't require perfect thoughts—just ones that move you closer to God's truth about your life. Each small shift in perspective builds momentum toward lasting change.

PRAYER
Gentle Father, guide me in transforming my thoughts one step at a time. When negative patterns surface, help me find bridge thoughts that lead to Your truth. Thank You for lighting my path toward positive change. Grant me patience with this process of renewal. Amen.

POSITIVE THOUGHT OF THE DAY
I take small steps toward positive thinking, trusting God's guidance.

August 29th

Finding the Middle Ground

SCRIPTURE
"The Lord is my shepherd; I shall not want. He makes me lie down in green pastures." - Psalm 23:1-2

REFLECTION
Like a shepherd guiding sheep across challenging terrain, God leads us gently through thought transformation. When overwhelmed by negative thoughts, we don't need to force artificial positivity. Instead, we can find middle-ground thoughts that feel authentic and hopeful. Start with simple additions like "I'm learning to..." or "It's possible that..." These gentle shifts create space for God's peace to enter our minds and hearts.

PRAYER
Lord of Wisdom, show me the gentle path between negativity and forced positivity. Help me find thoughts that honestly reflect both my struggles and Your hope. Thank You for Your patient guidance in transforming my mind. Lead me toward genuine positive thinking. Amen.

POSITIVE THOUGHT OF THE DAY
I choose thoughts that bridge me toward hope and peace.

August 30th

Growing in Truth

SCRIPTURE
"Finally, brothers and sisters, whatever is true, whatever is noble, whatever is right, whatever is pure, whatever is lovely, whatever is admirable—if anything is excellent or praiseworthy—think about such things." - Philippians 4:8

REFLECTION
Growth happens gradually, like climbing a ladder one rung at a time. When facing challenging situations, we can move from "Nothing ever works out" to "It's possible to find one thing that went well today." This isn't denying difficulties but choosing to notice God's presence even in hard times. Each small shift in perspective opens our eyes to more of His goodness around us.

PRAYER
Faithful God, help me notice Your presence in every situation. When negative thoughts overwhelm me, guide me toward truth one step at a time. Thank You for Your constant work in renewing my mind. Grant me wisdom to see Your goodness even in challenges. Amen.

POSITIVE THOUGHT OF THE DAY
I grow stronger as I focus on truth and goodness each day.

August 31st

Building Better Thoughts

SCRIPTURE
"Do not conform to the pattern of this world, but be transformed by the renewing of your mind." - Romans 12:2

REFLECTION
Transforming our thought patterns requires patient building, like constructing a bridge one plank at a time. When caught in negative thinking, we can add phrases like "yet" or "and it's okay" to create stepping stones toward hope. These small adjustments aren't about denying reality but about opening our hearts to God's perspective. Remember, He sees beyond our current struggles to the growth He's nurturing within us.

PRAYER
Patient Lord, guide me in building positive thought patterns that align with Your truth. When I struggle with negativity, help me find gentle ways to shift toward hope. Thank You for Your constant work in transforming my mind. Give me courage to keep building better thoughts. Amen.

POSITIVE THOUGHT OF THE DAY
I build positive thoughts one small step at a time.

September

September 1st

Finding Balance Through Truth

SCRIPTURE
"He is like a tree planted by streams of water that yields its fruit in its season, and its leaf does not wither. In all that he does, he prospers." - Psalm 1:3

REFLECTION
Balance isn't a destination to reach, but a state of being to cultivate. Like a tree drawing sustenance from living waters, we find stability not in perfect circumstances, but in our connection with God. Today, recognize that balance comes from within—it's a feeling we create through our thoughts and choices rather than external conditions. Remember, sometimes choosing temporary imbalance serves a greater purpose in God's plan for our lives.

PRAYER
Wise Father, help me understand that true balance flows from my relationship with You. When life feels overwhelming, remind me that peace comes from internal alignment with Your will, not perfect circumstances. Thank You for showing me that balance is created through my choices and perspective. Guide me to find stability in Your unchanging presence. Amen.

POSITIVE THOUGHT OF THE DAY
I create balance from within by aligning my heart with God's wisdom.

September 2nd

Wisdom in Decision Making

SCRIPTURE
"If any of you lacks wisdom, let him ask God, who gives generously to all without reproach, and it will be given him." - James 1:5

REFLECTION
Strong decisions build the foundation for a balanced life. When we remain stuck in indecision, we create confusion that clouds our path. Today, practice making clear choices with confidence, trusting that God's wisdom guides us. Remember that taking action, even imperfect action, teaches us more than endless deliberation. Each decision moves us forward on our journey, helping us learn what serves our peace and what doesn't.

PRAYER
Lord of Wisdom, grant me clarity in my decisions and courage to act on them. When I feel stuck between choices, help me trust Your guidance. Thank You for teaching me through both successes and missteps. Give me strength to move forward with confidence in Your direction. Amen.

September 3rd

Nurturing Your Wellbeing

SCRIPTURE
"Or do you not know that your body is a temple of the Holy Spirit within you, whom you have from God? You are not your own, for you were bought with a price. So glorify God in your body." - 1 Corinthians 6:19-20

REFLECTION
Just as we can't pour from an empty cup, we can't sustain balance without tending to our wellbeing. God designed us with needs for rest, renewal, and spiritual nourishment. When we prioritize our mental and emotional health, we honor the temple He created. Today, recognize that caring for yourself isn't selfish—it's essential for serving others effectively and living out God's purpose for your life.

PRAYER
Loving Creator, help me value the importance of caring for my wellbeing. When I feel pulled in many directions, remind me to pause and restore my spirit. Thank You for designing me with needs for both work and rest. Guide me to honor these needs as I serve You and others. Amen.

POSITIVE THOUGHT OF THE DAY
I honor God by tending to my wellbeing with wisdom and care.

September 4th

Daily Drops of Wisdom

SCRIPTURE
"My son, do not forget my teaching, but keep my commands in your heart." - Proverbs 3:1

REFLECTION
Just as morning dew nourishes plants, small daily doses of wisdom refresh our spirits. Today, recognize that transformation doesn't require grand gestures—it comes through consistent moments of turning to God's truth. Whether in quiet morning moments or brief pauses throughout your day, these small investments in spiritual growth compound over time. Each moment spent in reflection helps reshape your thoughts and actions toward peace.

Lord of Wisdom, help me value small moments of connection with You. When life feels overwhelming, guide me to pause and drink from Your well of truth. Thank You for providing wisdom through Your word and through others. Grant me wisdom to make these brief encounters part of my daily rhythm. Amen.

POSITIVE THOUGHT OF THE DAY
I find strength in daily moments of wisdom and truth.

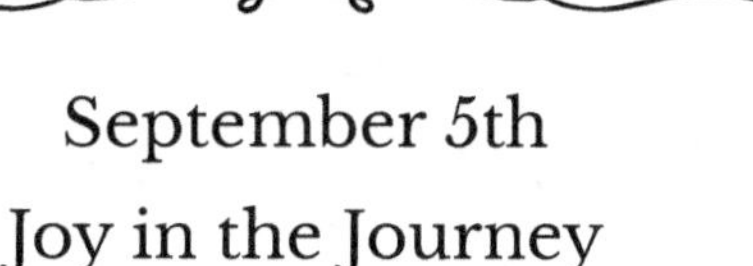

September 5th

Joy in the Journey

SCRIPTURE
"May the God of hope fill you with all joy and peace in believing, so that by the power of the Holy Spirit you may abound in hope." - Romans 15:13

REFLECTION
Life's beauty isn't reserved for perfect moments or accomplished goals—it's woven into each step of our journey. When we postpone joy until everything aligns perfectly, we miss countless opportunities for delight in the present. Today, look for moments of joy in ordinary places: a child's laughter, morning sunlight, or a quiet cup of coffee. These aren't distractions from life's challenges but divine invitations to experience God's presence.

PRAYER
Gracious Father, open my eyes to the joy available in each moment. Help me find delight in the journey rather than waiting for distant destinations. Thank You for filling ordinary moments with Your extraordinary presence. Guide me to notice and celebrate small blessings. Amen.

POSITIVE THOUGHT OF THE DAY
I choose joy in this moment, trusting God's presence in my journey.

September 6th

Organizing Heart and Mind

SCRIPTURE
"Create in me a clean heart, O God, and renew a right spirit within me." - Psalm 51:10

REFLECTION
Just as we organize our homes, our minds need regular attention and care. When thoughts become cluttered with worry and tasks, we can bring them to God for sorting and renewal. Today, practice bringing your scattered thoughts before Him—examine which ones serve your peace and which

need to be released. Let Him guide you in keeping thoughts that align with His truth and letting go of those that don't.

PRAYER
Divine Organizer, help me sort through the thoughts that fill my mind. When mental clutter overwhelms me, guide me in discerning which thoughts to keep and which to release. Thank You for offering clarity and peace. Lead me toward thoughts that align with Your truth. Amen.

POSITIVE THOUGHT OF THE DAY
I trust God to help me organize my thoughts and restore my peace.

September 7th

Growing in Patient Grace

SCRIPTURE
"Therefore, as God's chosen people, holy and dearly loved, clothe yourselves with compassion, kindness, humility, gentleness, and patience." - Colossians 3:12

REFLECTION
Patience grows not through external circumstances but through internal transformation. When we face moments that test our composure—a child's repeated questions, morning rushes, unexpected delays—these become opportunities for growth rather than sources of frustration. Today, notice when impatience rises and remember that these feelings aren't failures but invitations to practice extending grace to yourself and others.

PRAYER
Gentle Father, help me see challenging moments as opportunities for growth. When impatience rises, guide me to respond with grace rather than frustration. Thank You for Your endless patience with me. Grant me wisdom to extend that same patience to myself and others. Amen.

POSITIVE THOUGHT OF THE DAY
I respond to challenges with growing patience and grace.

September 8th

The Power of Perspective

SCRIPTURE
"Be joyful in hope, patient in affliction, faithful in prayer." - Romans 12:12

REFLECTION
How we view our circumstances shapes our response to them. When faced with delays or disruptions, we can choose to see them as obstacles or opportunities—chances to model flexibility, teach problem-solving, or

practice presence. Rather than letting unmet expectations fuel frustration, we can shift our focus to discovering unexpected blessings in these moments. Today, practice finding new perspectives in challenging situations.

PRAYER
Lord of Wisdom, help me see Your purpose in moments of waiting and challenge. When my plans are disrupted, guide me to find new possibilities rather than frustration. Thank You for showing me that every delay holds potential for growth. Grant me eyes to see beyond my immediate circumstances. Amen.

POSITIVE THOUGHT OF THE DAY
I choose to find opportunity in every challenge.

September 9th

Choosing Connection Over Control

SCRIPTURE
"Love is patient, love is kind. It does not envy, it does not boast, it is not proud." - 1 Corinthians 13:4

REFLECTION
True patience blooms when we prioritize relationships over rigid expectations. When we release our grip on perfect outcomes—whether in parenting, housekeeping, or daily schedules—we create space for meaningful connections. Today, when plans go awry, ask yourself: What matters more in this moment—perfection or connection? Let this guide your response and ease the burden of unrealistic expectations.

PRAYER
Loving Father, help me value connection above control. When I'm tempted to demand perfection, remind me of what truly matters. Thank You for showing me that relationships matter more than flawless execution. Guide me to choose love over rigid expectations. Amen.

POSITIVE THOUGHT OF THE DAY
I choose connection over control in each moment.

September 10th

Practicing Self-Compassion

SCRIPTURE
"The Lord is compassionate and gracious, slow to anger, abounding in love." - Psalm 103:8

Just as God extends endless patience to us, we're called to show compassion to ourselves. When we stumble in our pursuit of patience—losing our cool in traffic, sighing heavily at delays, or speaking sharply in stress—beating ourselves up only deepens the cycle. Instead, we can acknowledge our humanity, learn from these moments, and begin again with fresh grace. Today, practice treating yourself with the same patience you aim to show others.

PRAYER
Merciful God, help me extend to myself the same patience You show me. When I fall short of my ideals, guide me toward self-compassion rather than criticism. Thank You for Your endless grace in my journey of growth. Lead me to be gentle with myself as I learn and grow. Amen.

POSITIVE THOUGHT OF THE DAY
I respond to my shortcomings with patience and understanding.

September 11th

Finding Freedom in God's Truth

SCRIPTURE
"You formed my inmost being; you knit me in my mother's womb. I praise you, because I am wonderfully made; wonderful are your works!" - Psalm 139:13-14

REFLECTION
Our worth comes not from others' opinions but from our identity as God's beloved creation. When we focus on what others might think, we overlook the divine truth of who we are. Today, notice when you're seeking validation from outside sources rather than resting in God's unchanging love. Remember that He created you purposefully, knowing every detail of who you are and delighting in His handiwork.

PRAYER
Creator God, help me find my worth in Your love rather than others' opinions. When I'm tempted to seek external validation, draw me back to Your truth. Thank You for creating me with purpose and intention. Grant me confidence in my identity as Your beloved child. Amen.

POSITIVE THOUGHT OF THE DAY
I rest secure in God's love, not others' opinions.

September 12th

Living in Divine Freedom

SCRIPTURE
"The Lord is my light and my salvation; whom should I fear?" - Psalm 27:1

REFLECTION
Fear of judgment often keeps us from living fully in God's purpose for our lives. Like a bird hesitating to fly because others might watch, we limit ourselves through concern about others' thoughts. Today, recognize that while we can't control others' opinions, we can choose where to focus our attention. When we align our hearts with God's truth, others' judgments lose their power over us.

PRAYER
Lord of Freedom, release me from the chains of others' opinions. When I'm tempted to let fear of judgment guide my choices, anchor me in Your truth. Thank You for offering liberation through Your love. Help me walk confidently in the path You've set before me. Amen.

POSITIVE THOUGHT OF THE DAY
I choose to live freely in God's purpose, not others' expectations.

September 13th

Anchored in Truth

SCRIPTURE
"It is better to take refuge in the Lord than to put confidence in mortals."
- Psalm 118:8

REFLECTION
Just as a tree's strength comes from its roots, not others' opinions of its branches, our stability comes from being grounded in God's truth. When we spend energy imagining what others think, we drain ourselves of peace. Today, practice redirecting your focus from others' potential judgments to God's unchanging love and wisdom. Let His truth be the foundation that guides your choices and shapes your peace.

PRAYER
Faithful Father, help me anchor my confidence in Your truth rather than others' thoughts. When I'm caught up in worry about opinions, bring me back to Your unchanging love. Thank You for being my steady foundation. Guide me to find peace in Your perspective. Amen.

POSITIVE THOUGHT OF THE DAY
I find stability in God's truth, not others' opinions.

September 14th

Walking in Divine Confidence

SCRIPTURE
"Not that of ourselves we are qualified to take credit for anything as coming from us; rather, our qualification comes from God." - 2 Corinthians 3:5

REFLECTION
Our ability to parent well comes from God's grace, not others' approval. When we measure our worth by imagined opinions, we miss the divine confidence available to us. Today, rather than questioning what others might think, focus on the wisdom God provides. Remember that your qualifications as a mother come from His equipping, not others' validation.

PRAYER
Divine Guide, strengthen my confidence in the abilities You've given me. When I doubt myself based on others' potential judgments, remind me of Your qualification. Thank You for equipping me for this calling. Help me trust Your wisdom over others' opinions. Amen.

POSITIVE THOUGHT OF THE DAY
I walk confidently in God's calling, not others' approval.

September 15th

Present Joy in God's Love

SCRIPTURE
"Rejoice in the Lord always. I shall say it again: rejoice!" - Philippians 4:4

REFLECTION
True joy isn't found in future achievements but in our present relationship with God. When we postpone happiness until we reach certain milestones, we miss the gifts He offers today. Like waiting to open a present until tomorrow, we deny ourselves the joy available now. Today, notice where you're delaying happiness and choose instead to find delight in this moment—in your current circumstances, relationships, and blessings.

PRAYER
Lord of Joy, help me find happiness in this present moment. When I'm tempted to postpone joy until future achievements, remind me of Your presence now. Thank You for the gifts You've already given. Guide me to appreciate today's blessings while still working toward tomorrow's goals. Amen.

POSITIVE THOUGHT OF THE DAY
I choose to find joy in this moment, not just in future achievements.

September 16th

Gratitude's Path to Joy

SCRIPTURE
"Give thanks to the Lord for he is good, his mercy endures forever." - Psalm 107:1

REFLECTION
Gratitude opens our eyes to God's presence in every moment. When we focus solely on future goals, we blind ourselves to current blessings. Like a garden we forget to tend while dreaming of future harvests, we neglect the beauty already blooming in our lives. Today, cultivate thankfulness for what is, rather than waiting for what might be. Let appreciation for present gifts nurture your heart's contentment.

PRAYER
Gracious Father, open my eyes to Your gifts in this moment. When I'm caught up in future dreams, help me notice present blessings. Thank You for Your constant provision. Lead me to find joy through gratitude for what is, even as I work toward what will be. Amen.

POSITIVE THOUGHT OF THE DAY
I nurture joy through gratitude for today's gifts.

September 17th

SCRIPTURE
"The Lord is my shepherd; there is nothing I shall want." - Psalm 23:1

Contentment in God's Care

REFLECTION
Contentment grows from trusting God's provision in each moment. When we believe happiness awaits at some future milestone, we miss His care today. Like children too focused on dessert to enjoy their meal, we overlook the nourishment He provides now. Today, practice finding satisfaction in current circumstances while maintaining hope for future growth. Let trust in His shepherding bring peace to your present journey.

PRAYER
Divine Shepherd, help me trust Your provision for today. When I'm tempted to seek happiness only in future achievements, remind me of Your present care. Thank You for tending to my needs at each moment. Grant me contentment in Your timing and ways. Amen.

POSITIVE THOUGHT OF THE DAY
I find peace in God's provision for today.

September 18th

Joy in the Journey

SCRIPTURE
"This is the day the Lord has made; let us rejoice and be glad in it." - Psalm 118:24

REFLECTION
Each day holds opportunities for joy when we align our hearts with God's timing. Rather than postponing happiness until we reach certain goals, we can choose to celebrate small victories and find delight in daily moments. Like pilgrims who sing along their journey rather than waiting to rejoice at their destination, we can find joy in both our progress and our present place.

PRAYER
Lord of Each Moment, help me find joy in today's journey. When I'm fixated on future achievements, guide me to appreciate present progress. Thank You for walking beside me each step of the way. Grant me wisdom to celebrate both where I am and where I'm going. Amen.

POSITIVE THOUGHT OF THE DAY
I choose joy in the journey, not just the destination.

September 19th

Free From the Burden of Guilt

SCRIPTURE
"Therefore, there is now no condemnation for those who are in Christ Jesus." - Romans 8:1

REFLECTION
Guilt often masquerades as a measure of good motherhood, but it actually diminishes our effectiveness and drains our joy. Like carrying unnecessary weights while trying to run a race, guilt slows our progress and exhausts our strength. Today, recognize that feeling guilty doesn't make you a better mother—it only prevents you from being fully present. Let God's grace, not guilt, guide your parenting choices.

PRAYER
Merciful Father, release me from the burden of unnecessary guilt. When I feel inadequate, remind me that Your grace is sufficient. Thank You for loving me unconditionally. Help me parent from a place of peace rather than pressure. Amen.

POSITIVE THOUGHT OF THE DAY
I choose to parent from God's grace, not guilt.

September 20th

Grace in Our Limitations

SCRIPTURE
"My grace is sufficient for you, for power is made perfect in weakness." - 2 Corinthians 12:9

REFLECTION
Our limitations aren't failures—they're invitations to rely on God's strength. When we feel guilty about not meeting impossible standards, we miss opportunities to model grace and authenticity for our children. Today, practice adjusting expectations to align with reality rather than perfection. Remember that acknowledging our limits makes room for God's power to work through us.

PRAYER
Loving God, help me accept my human limitations with grace. When unrealistic expectations tempt me toward guilt, remind me of Your sufficiency. Thank You for working through my weakness. Guide me to parent within the boundaries You've wisely set. Amen.

POSITIVE THOUGHT OF THE DAY
I find freedom in accepting my limitations with grace.

September 21st

Quality in God's Presence

SCRIPTURE
"Better is one day in your courts than a thousand elsewhere." - Psalm 84:11

REFLECTION
Like a few drops of pure essential oil being more valuable than gallons of diluted mixture, the quality of our presence matters more than quantity of time. When guilt pushes us to fill every moment with activity, we miss opportunities for meaningful connection. Today, focus on being fully present in small moments rather than feeling guilty about time you can't give. Let each interaction be infused with love and attention.

PRAYER
Lord of Time, help me value quality over quantity in my relationships. When guilt tempts me to measure worth by minutes, guide me toward meaningful presence. Thank You for showing me that love isn't measured by time. Grant me wisdom to make each moment count. Amen.

POSITIVE THOUGHT OF THE DAY
I choose quality presence over quantity of time.

September 22nd

Strength in Community

SCRIPTURE
"Bear one another's burdens, and so fulfill the law of Christ." - Galatians 6:2

REFLECTION
God designed us to thrive in community, not struggle alone. When guilt tells us we should handle everything independently, we resist His plan for mutual support. Like branches drawing strength from the vine and each other, we grow stronger through connection. Today, recognize that asking for help isn't weakness—it's wisdom that allows us to serve our families better.

PRAYER
Divine Provider, give me courage to seek help when needed. When guilt whispers I should do it all alone, remind me of Your design for community. Thank You for placing supportive people in my life. Help me receive assistance with grace. Amen.

POSITIVE THOUGHT OF THE DAY
I find strength in accepting support from others.

September 23rd

Holy Boundaries

SCRIPTURE
"Let your 'Yes' mean 'Yes,' and your 'No' mean 'No.' Anything more is from the evil one." - Matthew 5:37

REFLECTION
Setting boundaries isn't selfish—it's stewardship of the time and energy God has given us. When we say yes to everything, we often end up saying no to what matters most. Like Jesus who withdrew from crowds despite endless needs, we too must discern when to engage and when to step back. Today, consider where you need to establish clearer boundaries to better serve God's priorities for your life.

PRAYER
Divine Guide, grant me wisdom to set healthy boundaries. When I'm tempted to overcommit, help me discern Your priorities. Thank You for showing me that limits can be loving. Give me courage to say no with grace when needed. Amen.

POSITIVE THOUGHT OF THE DAY
I honor God by setting healthy boundaries.

September 24th

Truth in Love

SCRIPTURE
"Speaking the truth in love, we are to grow up in every way into him who is the head, into Christ." - Ephesians 4:15

REFLECTION
Saying no with grace reflects Christ's example of speaking truth in love. When we fear disappointing others, we may compromise our authentic selves. Yet true relationships thrive on honesty, not people-pleasing. Today, practice speaking your truth with kindness, remembering that genuine love includes respectful limits. Let your yes and no flow from a place of integrity rather than fear.

PRAYER
Lord of Truth, help me communicate honestly and lovingly. When I'm afraid to disappoint others, remind me that authentic relationships require truth. Thank You for modeling perfect love. Guide me to express my boundaries with both firmness and grace. Amen.

POSITIVE THOUGHT OF THE DAY
I speak my truth with both kindness and clarity.

September 25th

Wisdom in Choice

SCRIPTURE
"If any of you lacks wisdom, let him ask God, who gives to all generously and without reproach, and it will be given him." - James 1:5

REFLECTION
Every yes carries hidden nos, and every no makes room for deeper yeses. Just as Mary chose the "better portion" by sitting at Jesus' feet, we too must discern what deserves our time and energy. Today, before responding to requests, pause to seek God's wisdom. Remember that saying no to good things creates space for God's best things in your life.

PRAYER
Wise Father, help me discern which commitments truly align with Your will. When decisions arise, grant me clarity to choose well. Thank You for guiding my choices. Lead me to say yes to what matters most. Amen.

POSITIVE THOUGHT OF THE DAY
I choose wisely, guided by God's wisdom.

September 26th

Peace in Priority

SCRIPTURE
"Seek first the kingdom of God and his righteousness, and all these things will be given you besides." - Matthew 6:33

REFLECTION
Setting priorities isn't about doing less—it's about doing what matters most. When we align our choices with God's purposes, peace follows. Like a garden that thrives with proper pruning, our lives flourish when we remove what doesn't serve our divine calling. Today, examine your commitments through the lens of God's priorities for your life.

PRAYER
Lord of Peace, help me align my priorities with Your purposes. When obligations overwhelm me, guide me to focus on what truly matters. Thank You for showing me that boundaries bring freedom. Grant me courage to live according to Your priorities. Amen.

POSITIVE THOUGHT OF THE DAY
I find peace in living according to God's priorities.

September 27th

Growing in God's Gentleness

SCRIPTURE
"For God did not give us a spirit of cowardice but rather of power and love and self-control." - 2 Timothy 1:7

REFLECTION
Self-criticism often masquerades as virtue, but God calls us to gentleness—with others and ourselves. Like a garden that needs both sunshine and rain to flourish, our spirits need both challenge and compassion to grow. Today, notice moments of harsh self-judgment and practice extending to yourself the same grace God so freely gives. Remember that you are His beloved child, created with purpose and cherished despite imperfections.

PRAYER
Gentle Father, help me treat myself with the kindness You show me. When I'm tempted toward harsh self-judgment, remind me of Your endless grace. Thank You for loving me completely. Guide me to see myself through Your eyes of compassion. Amen.

POSITIVE THOUGHT OF THE DAY
I extend to myself the same grace God gives me.

September 28th

Strength in Self-Kindness

SCRIPTURE
"She is clothed with strength and dignity, and laughs at the days to come."
- Proverbs 31:25

REFLECTION
True strength flows not from perfectionism but from accepting our humanity with grace. When we treat our mistakes as opportunities for growth rather than proof of failure, we align with God's vision for our lives. Today, practice responding to your shortcomings with understanding rather than criticism. Let each challenge become a stepping stone toward growth rather than a stumbling block of shame.

PRAYER
Lord of Wisdom, teach me to respond to myself with understanding. When I stumble, help me remember that growth comes through grace, not criticism. Thank You for seeing my potential beyond my mistakes. Lead me toward genuine self-kindness. Amen.

POSITIVE THOUGHT OF THE DAY
I grow stronger through self-kindness and understanding.

September 29th

Learning Through Love

SCRIPTURE
"Love is patient, love is kind... it is not irritable or resentful." - 1 Corinthians 13:4-5

REFLECTION
Just as love for others should be patient and kind, so should our love for ourselves. When we withhold compassion from ourselves, we limit our capacity to grow and serve. Today, practice treating yourself as you would a dear friend facing similar challenges. Remember that being human means learning through both successes and setbacks. Let patience with yourself become a form of worship.

PRAYER
Loving God, help me extend to myself the same patience I offer others. When I feel discouraged by my imperfections, remind me that growth comes through love. Thank You for Your patient guidance. Teach me to love myself as You love me. Amen.

POSITIVE THOUGHT OF THE DAY
I learn and grow through patient self-love.

September 30th

Complete in Christ

SCRIPTURE
"I give praise to you, for I am fearfully and wonderfully made. Wonderful are your works!" - Psalm 139:14

REFLECTION
Our worth comes not from perfect performance but from being God's beloved creation. Like a masterpiece that includes both light and shadow, our lives are meant to reflect His glory through both strengths and weaknesses. Today, resist measuring yourself against impossible standards. Instead, remember that you are complete in Christ, fully loved and worthy of compassion—not because of what you do, but because of whose you are.

PRAYER
Creator God, help me see my worth through Your eyes. When I'm tempted to measure myself harshly, remind me that I am Your beloved creation. Thank You for making me exactly as I am. Guide me to treat myself with the reverence due Your handiwork. Amen.

POSITIVE THOUGHT OF THE DAY
I am complete and worthy of compassion in Christ.

October

October 1st

Trusting God's Provision

SCRIPTURE
"Cast your cares upon the Lord and he will sustain you; never will he permit the just man to be disturbed." - Psalm 55:23

REFLECTION
Our relationship with money often reveals our deeper trust in God's provision. When we focus on numbers alone, we miss the spiritual dimension of stewardship. Today, examine whether worry about finances overshadows your faith in God's care. Remember that while practical management matters, true abundance flows from aligning our hearts with God's wisdom. Let your financial decisions become prayers of trust.

PRAYER
Provider God, help me trust Your abundance more than earthly wealth. When financial worries arise, guide me toward Your wisdom and peace. Thank You for Your faithful provision. Grant me grace to manage resources with both faith and prudence. Amen.

POSITIVE THOUGHT OF THE DAY
I trust in God's provision while managing resources wisely.

October 2nd

Peace Beyond Numbers

SCRIPTURE
"But seek first the kingdom of God and his righteousness, and all these things will be given you besides." - Matthew 6:33

REFLECTION
Financial peace flows not from perfect circumstances but from perfect trust. Like Martha distracted by many concerns, we often let money worries cloud our vision of God's faithfulness. Today, shift your focus from anxiety about numbers to confidence in God's care. Remember that while we steward earthly resources, our true wealth lies in our relationship with Him.

PRAYER
Lord of Peace, help me find serenity beyond financial circumstances. When money concerns overwhelm me, draw my heart back to Your promises. Thank You for providing all I truly need. Guide me to seek Your kingdom first in all things. Amen.

POSITIVE THOUGHT OF THE DAY
I choose peace in God's provision over financial worry.

October 3rd

Growing in Abundance

SCRIPTURE
"I came so that they might have life and have it more abundantly." - John 10:10

REFLECTION
God desires abundance for His children—not just in finances, but in faith, peace, and purpose. When we align our financial practices with spiritual wisdom, we open ourselves to receive His blessings fully. Today, consider how your money management reflects your trust in God's generous nature. Let your financial choices become expressions of faith rather than fear.

PRAYER
Generous Father, help me embrace Your vision of abundance. When scarcity thinking limits me, expand my trust in Your provision. Thank You for desiring my flourishing. Lead me to manage resources in ways that honor Your generosity. Amen.

POSITIVE THOUGHT OF THE DAY
I open my heart to God's abundant blessings.

October 4th

Divine Partnership

SCRIPTURE
"Honor the Lord with your wealth, with first fruits of all your produce." - Proverbs 3:9

REFLECTION
Managing money becomes sacred when we see it as partnership with God. Each financial decision can be an opportunity to express trust and gratitude for His provision. Today, view your resources through the lens of stewardship rather than ownership. Remember that everything we have comes from God's hand—our role is to manage it wisely for His glory.

PRAYER
Divine Partner, help me see money management as sacred stewardship. When handling finances, remind me that all belongs to You. Thank You for trusting me with resources. Guide me to use them according to Your wisdom. Amen.

POSITIVE THOUGHT OF THE DAY
I partner with God in managing His resources.

October 5th

Morning's Sacred Ground

SCRIPTURE
"Morning after morning he opens my ear that I may hear." - Isaiah 50:4

REFLECTION
Like morning dew preparing the earth for a new day, evening preparation creates space for grace to flourish. When we thoughtfully plan ahead, we make room for God's presence in our morning moments. Today, consider how evening preparation can become a prayer—an act of creating sacred space for tomorrow's blessings. Let each preparatory action become an invitation for divine peace to enter your morning rhythm.

PRAYER
Lord of Every Morning, help me prepare wisely for each new day. When evening comes, guide me to create space for tomorrow's grace. Thank You for the gift of new beginnings. Lead me to establish rhythms that welcome Your presence. Amen.

POSITIVE THOUGHT OF THE DAY
I prepare with purpose, making space for God's peace.

October 6th

First Fruits of Time

SCRIPTURE
"But seek first the kingdom of God and his righteousness, and all these things will be given you besides." - Matthew 6:33

REFLECTION
Giving God our first moments mirrors the biblical principle of first fruits. When we prioritize our spiritual preparation before daily demands begin, we align our hearts with divine purpose. Today, consider how you might offer your earliest moments to God—whether through prayer, scripture, or quiet reflection. Remember that self-care rooted in spiritual connection bears fruit throughout your day.

PRAYER
Divine Guide, help me dedicate my first moments to You. When busyness tempts me to rush past our time together, remind me to pause and connect. Thank You for meeting me in these quiet moments. Grant me wisdom to begin each day in Your presence. Amen.

POSITIVE THOUGHT OF THE DAY
I honor God with the first moments of my day.

October 7th

Setting a Holy Tone

SCRIPTURE
"This is the day the Lord has made; let us rejoice and be glad in it." - Psalm 118:24

REFLECTION
Each morning offers a fresh opportunity to set a tone that reflects God's joy. Like a conductor leading an orchestra, we can intentionally create an atmosphere that uplifts our family's spirits. Whether through music, prayer, or shared gratitude, our chosen "morning vibe" can transform routine moments into occasions for grace. Today, consider how your morning atmosphere might better reflect God's presence.

PRAYER
Creator God, help me establish a morning atmosphere that honors You. When chaos threatens to overshadow peace, guide me back to Your rhythm. Thank You for the gift of each new day. Lead me in creating moments that reflect Your joy. Amen.

POSITIVE THOUGHT OF THE DAY
I choose to create mornings filled with God's peace and joy.

October 8th

Grace in Every Season

SCRIPTURE
"He has made everything beautiful in its time." - Ecclesiastes 3:11

REFLECTION
Life's seasons bring changing rhythms to our mornings—from newborn nights to school-day rushes to quiet empty nests. Rather than seeking perfect routines, we can embrace God's grace in each season's unique flow. Today, remember that some mornings will flow smoothly while others test our patience. In both, God's presence remains constant, offering peace amid imperfection.

PRAYER
Lord of All Seasons, help me find Your grace in each morning's rhythm. When routines feel challenging, remind me of Your constant presence. Thank You for walking with me through every season. Guide me to accept both smooth and difficult mornings with trust. Amen.

POSITIVE THOUGHT OF THE DAY
I welcome God's grace in every morning season.

October 9th

Joy in Simple Moments

SCRIPTURE
"Rejoice in the Lord always. I shall say it again: rejoice!" - Philippians 4:4

REFLECTION
Joy often hides in life's ordinary moments, waiting to be discovered through eyes of faith. Like hidden treasure in a familiar field, God plants moments of delight within our daily routines. When we release the need for perfect circumstances or grand occasions, we find His gifts in a child's smile, morning sunlight, or shared meals. Today, practice noticing these small graces woven through your everyday moments.

PRAYER
Gracious Father, open my eyes to Your gifts in ordinary moments. When I'm tempted to overlook simple joys, help me pause and notice Your presence. Thank You for filling each day with hidden blessings. Guide me to discover joy in life's simple moments. Amen.

POSITIVE THOUGHT OF THE DAY
I find God's joy in life's simple moments.

October 10th

Present to Grace

SCRIPTURE
"This is the day the Lord has made; let us rejoice and be glad in it." - Psalm 118:24

REFLECTION
Being fully present allows us to experience God's grace in each moment. When we set aside distractions and perfectionism, we create space to notice divine fingerprints in our daily lives. Like Mary choosing "the better portion" at Jesus' feet, we too can choose to be present to the holy moments within our ordinary days. Today, practice giving your full attention to the present moment, trusting that God's joy awaits your notice.

PRAYER
Lord of Each Moment, help me stay present to Your grace. When distractions pull me from joy, draw me back to Now. Thank You for filling each moment with Your presence. Guide me to choose presence over perfection. Amen.

POSITIVE THOUGHT OF THE DAY
I choose presence over distraction to find God's joy.

October 11th

Freedom in Simplicity

SCRIPTURE
"My grace is sufficient for you, for power is made perfect in weakness." - 2 Corinthians 12:9

REFLECTION
Joy flourishes in the soil of simplicity. When we release the burden of overcommitment and perfectionism, we create room for delight to grow. Like a garden that thrives with proper pruning, our lives bloom more beautifully when we remove what crowds out joy. Today, consider what you might need to release to make more space for God's simple gifts in your life.

PRAYER
Divine Gardener, help me cultivate simplicity in my life. When I'm tempted toward excess, guide me toward what truly matters. Thank You for showing me that less can lead to more joy. Lead me to choose what brings life and peace. Amen.

POSITIVE THOUGHT OF THE DAY
I find freedom and joy in choosing simplicity.

October 12th

Gratitude's Gift

SCRIPTURE
"Give thanks to the Lord for he is good, his mercy endures forever." - Psalm 107:1

REFLECTION
Gratitude opens our eyes to joy already present in our lives. When we shift from focusing on what's missing to appreciating what we have, we discover countless moments of grace. Like morning dew reflecting sunlight, gratitude helps us see God's glory in everyday moments. Today, practice intentional thankfulness, noting the small blessings that might otherwise go unnoticed.

PRAYER
Generous God, help me cultivate a heart of gratitude. When negativity clouds my vision, remind me to count Your blessings. Thank You for countless gifts in each day. Guide me to notice and celebrate Your goodness. Amen.

POSITIVE THOUGHT OF THE DAY
I choose gratitude to discover daily joy.

October 13th

Small Steps of Stewardship

SCRIPTURE
"Whatever you do, do from the heart, as for the Lord and not for others."
- Colossians 3:23

REFLECTION
Just as God created the world in small, orderly steps, we too can bring order to our homes through small, intentional actions. Each tiny effort—organizing a drawer while coffee brews, straightening a shelf while dinner cooks—becomes an act of stewardship when done with love. Today, look for small moments to create order, remembering that faithful stewardship often happens in life's ordinary moments.

PRAYER
Lord, help me see small opportunities to create beauty and peace. When tasks seem overwhelming, remind me that little steps matter. Thank You for the gift of each moment to serve. Guide me to be faithful in small things. Amen.

POSITIVE THOUGHT OF THE DAY
I create order through small, faithful actions.

October 14th

Rhythms of Grace

SCRIPTURE
"To everything there is a season, and a time for every purpose under heaven." - Ecclesiastes 3:1

REFLECTION
God wove rhythms into creation—day and night, seasons, tides. Similarly, our homes thrive when we establish gentle routines rather than seeking dramatic transformations. Like daily prayer that shapes our spiritual life, small organizing habits create lasting order. Today, consider what simple rhythms might bring more peace to your home and heart.

PRAYER
Divine Creator, help me establish life-giving routines in my home. When I'm tempted toward overwhelming projects, guide me to sustainable rhythms. Thank You for modeling order through Your creation. Lead me to patterns that bring peace. Amen.

POSITIVE THOUGHT OF THE DAY
I find peace in steady, sustainable routines.

October 15th

Spaces of Grace

SCRIPTURE
"By wisdom a house is built, and through understanding it is established."
- Proverbs 24:3

REFLECTION
Creating spaces that nurture our spirits reflects God's care in designing sacred spaces. Like the temple's careful arrangement to foster worship, we can organize our homes to support prayer, rest, and family connection. Today, consider how you might create one small space that invites peace and prayer—a corner for morning devotions or evening reflection.

PRAYER
Master Designer, guide me in creating spaces that nurture peace. When chaos threatens, help me maintain islands of calm. Thank You for teaching me the importance of sacred space. Show me how to make room for Your presence. Amen.

POSITIVE THOUGHT OF THE DAY
I create spaces that welcome God's peace.

October 16th

Order from Love

SCRIPTURE
"Let all things be done decently and in order." - 1 Corinthians 14:40

REFLECTION
True order flows from love, not perfectionism. When we organize our homes with hearts focused on serving family and fostering peace, the task becomes ministry rather than burden. Like Martha learning to balance service with presence, we can create order while keeping our hearts centered on what matters most. Today, let love guide your organizing efforts.

PRAYER
Loving Father, help me create order from a heart of service. When tasks overwhelm me, remind me of their deeper purpose. Thank You for showing me that organization can be ministry. Guide me to balance order with presence. Amen.

POSITIVE THOUGHT OF THE DAY
I create order as an expression of love.

October 17th

Evening's Sacred Rhythms

SCRIPTURE
"When you lie down, you will not be afraid; when you lie down, your sleep will be sweet." - Proverbs 3:24

REFLECTION
Just as God established evening's gentle transition from day to night, we too can create peaceful rhythms for our families. Rather than viewing evening routines as a race to finish, we can transform them into sacred moments of connection and rest. Today, consider how your evening routine might better reflect God's design for rest and renewal. Let each step become a prayer of gratitude and transition.

PRAYER
Lord of Evening Peace, help me create gentle rhythms for my family. When chaos threatens our evenings, guide me toward Your peace. Thank You for the gift of daily transitions. Lead me in establishing routines that honor rest. Amen.

POSITIVE THOUGHT OF THE DAY
I create evening rhythms that welcome God's peace.

October 18th

Grace in Transitions

SCRIPTURE
"The Lord is my shepherd; there is nothing I shall want. In verdant pastures he gives me repose." - Psalm 23:1-2

REFLECTION
Like a shepherd guiding his flock to evening rest, God calls us to lead our families with gentle wisdom. Each evening transition—from activity to rest, from noise to quiet—offers opportunities to practice patience and grace. Today, notice where evening stress reveals needs for adjustment. Remember that even small changes, made with love, can transform our family's evening peace.

PRAYER
Divine Shepherd, guide me in leading my family toward evening peace. When transitions feel challenging, help me respond with grace. Thank You for showing me areas that need attention. Grant me wisdom to make gentle changes. Amen.

POSITIVE THOUGHT OF THE DAY
I guide my family toward peace with patient love.

October 19th

Finding Holy Order

SCRIPTURE
"God called the light 'day,' and the darkness he called 'night.' And there was evening, and there was morning." - Genesis 1:5

REFLECTION
God established order from the beginning, separating day from night with purpose and care. When we thoughtfully plan our evenings, we participate in this divine ordering of time. Like arranging stones to create a path, each intentional choice in our evening routine helps guide our families toward rest. Today, examine your evening patterns with compassion, seeking ways to reflect God's orderly love.

PRAYER
Creator God, help me establish evening routines that honor Your order. When chaos threatens, remind me of Your patient ways. Thank You for modeling purposeful transitions. Guide me in creating paths to peace. Amen.

POSITIVE THOUGHT OF THE DAY
I create order that leads my family toward peace.

October 20th

Rest in His Care

SCRIPTURE
"It is vain for you to rise early and put off your rest at night, to eat bread earned by hard toil—all this God gives to his beloved in sleep." - Psalm 127:2

REFLECTION
True evening peace flows not from perfect execution but from trust in God's care. Like children who rest secure in their parents' love, we can release anxiety about evening routines and trust God's grace to fill our gaps. Today, practice releasing perfectionism about evening schedules, remembering that God's presence matters more than flawless performance.

PRAYER
Loving Father, help me trust Your care as evening approaches. When I worry about perfect routines, remind me of Your sufficient grace. Thank You for watching over our family's rest. Guide us toward peaceful surrender to Your care. Amen.

POSITIVE THOUGHT OF THE DAY
I trust God's care as evening falls.

October 21st

Morning's Sacred Energy

SCRIPTURE
"O Lord, in the morning I will direct my prayer to You, and I will look up." - Psalm 5:3

REFLECTION
Just as dawn gradually illuminates the day, our morning practices set the tone for our energy. Starting with meditation or prayer creates space for God's strength to fill us before demands begin. Like gathering manna in the desert, these early moments of collecting spiritual energy sustain us through our day. Today, consider how your first moments might better align with receiving God's strength.

PRAYER
Lord of Morning Light, help me begin each day in Your presence. When busyness tempts me to rush past our time together, remind me that You are my true source of energy. Thank You for offering fresh strength each morning. Guide me to start my days in ways that honor You. Amen.

POSITIVE THOUGHT OF THE DAY
I begin each day by drawing strength from God.

October 22nd

Creation's Renewing Power

SCRIPTURE
"The heavens declare the glory of God; the skies proclaim the work of his hands." - Psalm 19:1

REFLECTION
God's creation offers natural sources of renewal—sunlight for vitamin D, fresh air for clarity, movement for vigor. When we step outside amid His handiwork, we tap into divine energizing power. Like plants turning toward sunlight, our bodies and spirits naturally revive in nature's presence. Today, seek moments to experience God's invigorating creation, whether through a midday walk or quiet moments in sunlight.

PRAYER
Creator God, help me find renewal in Your natural world. When fatigue weighs me down, guide me to Your refreshing creation. Thank You for providing natural sources of energy. Lead me to recognize and use these gifts wisely. Amen.

POSITIVE THOUGHT OF THE DAY
I find renewal in God's creation.

October 23rd

Temple Care

SCRIPTURE
"Do you not know that your body is a temple of the holy Spirit within you, whom you have from God?" - 1 Corinthians 6:19

REFLECTION
Caring for our physical bodies—through water, nourishment, and movement—becomes an act of worship when done mindfully. Each choice to tend our "temple" through healthy practices honors God's design. Like maintaining a sacred space, these small acts of stewardship compound into greater energy and capacity to serve. Today, view your physical care choices as opportunities for reverence.

PRAYER
Divine Designer, help me honor Your temple through wise care. When I'm tempted to neglect physical stewardship, remind me this body is Your gift. Thank You for creating me with needs that draw me closer to You. Guide me in caring choices that glorify You. Amen.

POSITIVE THOUGHT OF THE DAY
I honor God by caring for my body's needs.

October 24th

Holy Connection

SCRIPTURE
"Iron sharpens iron, and one person sharpens another." - Proverbs 27:17

REFLECTION
God designed us for connection—with Him and others. When we engage in uplifting conversation or join in faith community, we tap into energy beyond ourselves. Like coals that grow brighter together, shared faith and friendship multiply our strength. Today, seek energy-giving connections, whether through prayer groups, spiritual friendship, or worship community.

PRAYER
God of Community, help me find strength through holy connections. When isolation tempts me, guide me toward life-giving relationships. Thank You for providing spiritual companions for the journey. Lead me to connections that build up faith and energy. Amen.

POSITIVE THOUGHT OF THE DAY
I find energy through spiritual connection.

October 25th

Scripture's Living Power

SCRIPTURE
"Your word is a lamp for my feet, a light for my path." - Psalm 119:105

REFLECTION
God's Word provides constant renewable energy for our spirits. When we pause to read scripture, we plug into divine power that refreshes and sustains. Like a steady stream of living water, regular scripture reading maintains our spiritual vitality. Today, make time to drink from this bottomless well of strength, whether through morning meditation or midday renewal.

PRAYER
Word of Life, energize me through Your sacred scripture. When weariness clouds my mind, refresh me through Your truth. Thank You for providing endless spiritual nourishment. Guide me to drink deeply from Your Word each day. Amen.

POSITIVE THOUGHT OF THE DAY
I find energy in God's living Word.

October 26th

Rest as Holy Rhythm

SCRIPTURE
"Come to me, all you who labor and are burdened, and I will give you rest." - Matthew 11:28

REFLECTION
God wove rest into creation's fabric—through night and day, seasons, and Sabbath. When we honor these rhythms of rest, we align with His design for sustained energy. Like machines that need regular maintenance, our bodies and spirits require consistent renewal. Today, embrace God's gift of rest, knowing it multiplies our capacity to serve.

PRAYER
Lord of Rest, help me honor Your rhythms of renewal. When busyness tempts me to ignore rest, remind me of Your wisdom in creating these patterns. Thank You for providing regular restoration. Guide me to accept and use these gifts of rest. Amen.

POSITIVE THOUGHT OF THE DAY
I find energy through holy rest.

October 27th

Gratitude's Power

SCRIPTURE
"Give thanks to the Lord for he is good, his mercy endures forever." - Psalm 107:1

REFLECTION
Gratitude generates spiritual energy by aligning our hearts with God's goodness. When we pause to count blessings, we tap into divine power that lifts and sustains. Like turning on a light in darkness, gratitude illuminates God's presence and revives our spirits. Today, intentionally notice and thank God for His gifts, allowing appreciation to energize your spirit.

PRAYER
Generous Father, help me find energy through thankfulness. When fatigue dims my vision, brighten my perspective through gratitude. Thank You for countless daily gifts that can renew my spirit. Guide me to notice and celebrate Your constant care. Amen.

POSITIVE THOUGHT OF THE DAY
I find energy through grateful praise.

October 28th

Daily Bread of PRAYER

SCRIPTURE
"Pray without ceasing." - 1 Thessalonians 5:17

REFLECTION
Prayer isn't a formal obligation but a lifeline connecting us to God's heart. Like children naturally sharing their days with loving parents, we're invited to bring every moment to our Heavenly Father. This connection sustains our spiritual growth and maturity. Today, view prayer not as a task to complete but as ongoing conversation with One who deeply loves you. Let each moment become an opportunity for connection.

PRAYER
Loving Father, help me grow in consistent prayer with You. When I overcomplicate our connection, remind me that You welcome simple conversation. Thank You for always listening. Guide me toward deeper daily communion with You. Amen.

POSITIVE THOUGHT OF THE DAY
I grow through daily conversation with God.

October 29th

Nourished by His Word

SCRIPTURE
"Your words were found, and I ate them, and your words became to me a joy and the delight of my heart." - Jeremiah 15:16

REFLECTION
God's Word provides essential nourishment for spiritual growth. Whether through reading, listening, or meditation, regular engagement with scripture shapes our maturity in faith. Like daily bread sustaining physical life, God's Word feeds our spirits. Today, consider how you might incorporate scripture into your daily rhythms, trusting that even small portions provide vital spiritual food.

PRAYER
Divine Teacher, help me hunger for Your Word. When busyness tempts me to skip spiritual nourishment, draw me back to Your truth. Thank You for providing living guidance. Lead me to find sustainable ways to feed on Your Word. Amen.

POSITIVE THOUGHT OF THE DAY
I grow stronger through God's living Word.

October 30th

Walking in Trust

SCRIPTURE
"Trust in the Lord with all your heart, and do not lean on your own understanding." - Proverbs 3:5

REFLECTION
Spiritual maturity grows through trusting God with life's details before seeing outcomes. When we release our need to control every aspect and result, we create space for divine wisdom to work. Like a child holding a parent's hand while walking in darkness, trust allows us to move forward with confidence. Today, practice releasing your grip on certainty, choosing instead to trust God's guidance.

PRAYER
Faithful Guide, strengthen my trust in Your care. When uncertainty tempts me to grasp for control, help me rest in Your wisdom. Thank You for Your trustworthy leadership. Grant me grace to follow without seeing the full path. Amen.

POSITIVE THOUGHT OF THE DAY
I grow in faith by trusting God's guidance.

October 31st

Spirit-Led Living

SCRIPTURE
"Since we live by the Spirit, let us keep in step with the Spirit." - Galatians 5:25

REFLECTION
The Holy Spirit desires to empower our daily lives, offering strength beyond our natural capacity. When we welcome divine assistance, ordinary moments transform into opportunities for supernatural grace. Like a sail catching wind, our lives move with greater purpose when yielded to the Spirit's power. Today, consciously invite the Holy Spirit's presence and guidance into each situation.

PRAYER
Holy Spirit, fill me with Your power for daily living. When I'm tempted to rely solely on my strength, remind me of Your presence. Thank You for Your constant help. Guide me to live in Your power moment by moment. Amen.

POSITIVE THOUGHT OF THE DAY
I grow stronger through the Holy Spirit's power.

November

November 1st

Holy Self-Care

SCRIPTURE
"Or do you not know that your body is a temple of the holy Spirit within you, whom you have from God, and that you are not your own?" - 1 Corinthians 6:19

REFLECTION
Caring for ourselves isn't selfish—it's sacred stewardship of God's temple. When we view self-care through the lens of faith, it becomes not an indulgence but a holy responsibility. Like tending a sanctuary, nurturing our physical, emotional, and spiritual wellbeing honors God's design. Today, consider how caring for yourself might become an act of worship rather than a source of guilt.

PRAYER
Divine Creator, help me see self-care as sacred stewardship. When guilt tempts me to neglect my needs, remind me that I care for Your temple. Thank You for entrusting me with this vessel. Guide me in tending it wisely. Amen.

POSITIVE THOUGHT OF THE DAY
I honor God by caring for His temple.

November 2nd

Rhythms of Grace

SCRIPTURE
"Come to me, all you who labor and are burdened, and I will give you rest." - Matthew 11:28

REFLECTION
Just as God wove rest into creation through day and night, seasons, and Sabbath, He invites us to establish sustainable rhythms of renewal. Like a garden that needs regular tending, our spirits thrive with consistent care. Today, consider what daily practices might nourish your soul and strengthen your capacity to serve others.

PRAYER
Lord of Rest, help me establish holy rhythms of renewal. When busyness threatens to overwhelm, draw me back to Your pattern of rest and work. Thank You for modeling balanced living. Guide me in creating sustainable self-care habits. Amen.

POSITIVE THOUGHT OF THE DAY
I grow stronger through consistent spiritual care.

November 3rd

Filled to Overflow

SCRIPTURE
"May the God of hope fill you with all joy and peace in believing, so that you may abound in hope by the power of the holy Spirit." - Romans 15:13

REFLECTION
We can only give from what we possess. Like a vessel that must be filled before it can pour out, we need regular replenishment to serve others effectively. When we maintain our spiritual, emotional, and physical reserves, we have more to share. Today, notice where your resources feel depleted and intentionally seek restoration.

PRAYER
Generous God, help me maintain fullness of spirit. When serving others depletes me, remind me to return to Your wellspring. Thank You for providing endless renewal. Guide me to stay filled with Your grace. Amen.

POSITIVE THOUGHT OF THE DAY
I serve best when filled with God's grace.

November 4th

Listening to Our Hearts

SCRIPTURE
"More than anything you guard, protect your mind, for life flows from it." - Proverbs 4:23

REFLECTION
Recognizing our needs requires holy attention to our hearts. When we regularly pause to check our spiritual and emotional wellbeing, we better steward the life God gave us. Like shepherds monitoring their flocks, we must stay attuned to signs that we need renewal. Today, practice listening to your heart's signals for rest, joy, or connection.

PRAYER
Wise Father, help me recognize when I need renewal. When I ignore signs of depletion, guide me back to awareness. Thank You for creating me with needs that draw me closer to You. Lead me in mindful self-care. Amen.

POSITIVE THOUGHT OF THE DAY
I honor God's wisdom by heeding my heart's needs.

November 5th

Grace in Our Humanity

SCRIPTURE
"The Lord is gracious and merciful, slow to anger and abounding in steadfast love." - Psalm 145:8

REFLECTION
Just as God shows patience with our humanity, we're called to extend grace to ourselves when emotions overflow. Like waves that occasionally surge beyond their usual boundaries, our feelings sometimes overflow their banks. Rather than condemning these moments, we can view them as opportunities to practice self-compassion and growth. Today, remember that being human means experiencing the full range of emotions while remaining anchored in God's love.

PRAYER
Merciful Father, help me accept my human emotions with grace. When I fall short of my ideals, remind me of Your patient love. Thank You for understanding my humanity. Guide me toward gentle self-acceptance. Amen.

POSITIVE THOUGHT OF THE DAY
I respond to my emotions with God's grace.

November 6th

Understanding Our Hearts

SCRIPTURE
"Above all else, guard your heart, for everything you do flows from it." - Proverbs 4:23

REFLECTION
Understanding our emotions requires holy attention and wisdom. When we take time to name and examine our feelings, we partner with God in the journey of self-awareness. Like a shepherd knowing each sheep, we must learn to recognize our emotional patterns and their origins. Today, practice pausing to identify your feelings, remembering that awareness is the first step toward transformation.

PRAYER
Divine Teacher, help me understand my emotional landscape. When strong feelings arise, guide me to pause and reflect. Thank You for creating me with depth of feeling. Lead me in managing emotions wisely. Amen.

POSITIVE THOUGHT OF THE DAY
I grow in wisdom by understanding my emotions.

November 7th

Friendship with Self

SCRIPTURE
"As I have loved you, so you also should love one another." - John 13:34

REFLECTION
God's love teaches us how to befriend ourselves in difficult moments. When emotions overwhelm, we can practice speaking to ourselves with the same compassion we'd offer a dear friend. Like Christ who showed tenderness to those struggling, we can extend understanding to our own hearts. Today, practice being your own best friend, especially in moments of emotional challenge.

PRAYER
Loving God, help me treat myself with the kindness You show me. When I'm tempted toward harsh self-judgment, guide me to compassionate understanding. Thank You for modeling perfect love. Teach me to extend that love to myself. Amen.

POSITIVE THOUGHT OF THE DAY
I choose friendship with myself through God's love.

November 8th

Learning Through Love

SCRIPTURE
"There is no fear in love, but perfect love drives out fear." - 1 John 4:18

REFLECTION
Every emotional surge offers an opportunity for growth through love. When we approach our feelings with curiosity rather than condemnation, we create space for God's transforming grace. Like students learning valuable lessons, we can view emotional challenges as classrooms for spiritual growth. Today, practice seeing difficult emotions as teachers rather than enemies.

PRAYER
Patient Teacher, help me learn from every emotion. When feelings overwhelm me, guide me toward Your lessons. Thank You for using all

experiences for my growth. Lead me in learning through love rather than fear. Amen.

POSITIVE THOUGHT OF THE DAY
I grow through emotional challenges with God's help.

November 9th

Prayers in Small Moments

SCRIPTURE
"Pray without ceasing." - 1 Thessalonians 5:17

REFLECTION
God delights in every prayer, no matter how brief. Like drops of rain that nourish soil, even the shortest prayers water our spiritual lives. When life's pace feels overwhelming, we can still maintain connection through quick phrases like "Help me" or "Thank you, Lord." Today, practice offering these small spiritual moments to God, trusting that He treasures each brief connection.

PRAYER
Loving Father, help me find You in life's small moments. When busyness threatens to disconnect me, remind me that brief prayers matter. Thank You for welcoming every whispered word. Guide me in maintaining constant connection through simple prayers. Amen.

POSITIVE THOUGHT OF THE DAY
I connect with God through brief, sincere prayers.

November 10th

Trust in Moments

SCRIPTURE
"Trust in him at all times, you people; pour out your hearts before him; God is our refuge." - Psalm 62:9

REFLECTION
Each moment offers an opportunity to renew our trust in God. When challenges arise, simple prayers like "I trust You" or "Help my unbelief" anchor us in divine care. Like a child instinctively reaching for a parent's hand, we can reach toward God with these brief expressions of faith. Today, practice responding to uncertainty with quick prayers of trust.

PRAYER
Faithful God, strengthen my trust through simple prayers. When doubts arise, help me turn to You with brief words of faith. Thank You for hearing every whispered trust. Lead me to rely on You in all moments. Amen.

POSITIVE THOUGHT OF THE DAY
I grow in trust through simple prayers.

November 11th

Gratitude's Quick Grace

SCRIPTURE
"Give thanks to the Lord, for he is good, his love endures forever." - Psalm 107:1

REFLECTION
Brief prayers of thanks transform ordinary moments into occasions of grace. When we pause to whisper "Thank You" to God—for a child's smile, a quiet moment, even life's challenges—we align our hearts with His presence. Like collecting precious stones, these small moments of gratitude accumulate into treasure. Today, practice offering quick thanks throughout your day.

PRAYER
God of Grace, help me notice moments for gratitude. When blessings appear, guide me to pause in quick thanks. Thank You for receiving my briefest prayers. Lead me to grow in grateful awareness. Amen.

POSITIVE THOUGHT OF THE DAY
I find joy in quick prayers of thanks.

November 12th

Love's Brief Whispers

SCRIPTURE
"Because he loves me," says the Lord, "I will rescue him; I will protect him, for he acknowledges my name." - Psalm 91:14

REFLECTION
Simple expressions of love deepen our relationship with God. Just as we cherish quick "I love you's" from our children, God delights in our brief expressions of devotion. Like thread connecting pearls, these small moments of love create a beautiful pattern through our days. Today, practice offering God quick whispers of love amid life's activities.

PRAYER
Loving Lord, receive my brief expressions of love. When life moves quickly, help me pause to say "I love You." Thank You for cherishing every whispered word. Guide me in showing love through simple prayers. Amen.

POSITIVE THOUGHT OF THE DAY
I express love through brief prayers throughout my day.

November 13th

Choosing Peace Over Worry

SCRIPTURE
"Cast your care upon the Lord, who will give you support." - Psalm 55:23

REFLECTION
God invites us to exchange worry for trust. When anxiety tempts us to control everything, we can choose instead to place our concerns in divine hands. Like exchanging heavy stones for precious gems, we can trade worrying thoughts for peaceful trust. Today, practice catching moments of worry and deliberately choosing trust instead, remembering that God holds every detail of our lives.

PRAYER
Lord of Peace, help me choose trust over worry. When anxious thoughts arise, guide me toward Your peace. Thank You for carrying my concerns. Lead me to rest in Your care. Amen.

POSITIVE THOUGHT OF THE DAY
I choose God's peace over worry's weight.

November 14th

Clarity Through Faith

SCRIPTURE
"If any of you lacks wisdom, let him ask God, who gives to all generously and without reproach." - James 1:5

REFLECTION
Confusion dissolves in the light of God's wisdom. When we feel uncertain about decisions, we can turn to prayer rather than staying stuck in indecision. Like fog clearing in morning sunlight, divine guidance dispels our confusion when we seek it. Today, practice replacing confusion with confident seeking of God's direction, trusting that He provides the clarity we need.

PRAYER
Divine Guide, transform my confusion into clarity. When uncertainty paralyzes me, help me seek Your wisdom. Thank You for offering clear direction. Lead me in confident decision-making. Amen.

POSITIVE THOUGHT OF THE DAY
I find clarity through seeking God's wisdom.

November 15th

God's Perfect Love

SCRIPTURE
"Perfect love drives out fear, for fear has to do with punishment." - 1 John 4:18

REFLECTION
Self-doubt withers in the warmth of God's perfect love. When we question our worth or abilities, we can remember that we are divinely created and equipped for our calling. Like plants turning toward sunlight, our confidence grows when we focus on God's belief in us. Today, practice replacing self-doubt with awareness of God's complete love and confidence in you.

PRAYER
Loving Father, replace my doubts with trust in Your design. When I question my worth, remind me of Your perfect love. Thank You for believing in me completely. Guide me to see myself through Your eyes. Amen.

POSITIVE THOUGHT OF THE DAY
I stand confident in God's perfect love.

November 16th

Grace Over Guilt

SCRIPTURE
"Where sin increased, grace overflowed all the more." - Romans 5:20

REFLECTION
God offers grace in place of guilt. When we're tempted to carry heavy burdens of self-condemnation, He invites us to receive His forgiveness and move forward in freedom. Like trading chains for wings, we can exchange guilt for the lightness of grace. Today, practice choosing God's grace over guilt's weight, remembering that His love lifts our burdens.

PRAYER
God of Grace, help me release guilt and receive Your mercy. When self-condemnation weighs me down, lift me with Your love. Thank You for offering freedom through grace. Guide me to live in Your forgiveness. Amen.

POSITIVE THOUGHT OF THE DAY
I choose God's grace over guilt's burden.

November 17th

Freedom in Acceptance

SCRIPTURE
"Accept one another, then, just as Christ accepted you, in order to bring praise to God." - Romans 15:7

REFLECTION
Just as God accepts us without requiring perfection, we're called to release rigid expectations of others. When we hold mental "instruction manuals" for how others should behave, we create our own suffering. Like trying to control the wind, attempting to manage others only leads to frustration. Today, practice accepting others as they are, remembering that God's love embraces us in our imperfection.

PRAYER
Merciful Father, help me release my expectations of others. When I'm tempted to control, remind me of Your accepting love. Thank You for accepting me as I am. Guide me to extend that same grace to others. Amen.

POSITIVE THOUGHT OF THE DAY
I find peace in accepting others as they are.

November 18th

Love Without Demands

SCRIPTURE
"Love is patient, love is kind... It does not insist on its own way." - 1 Corinthians 13:4-5

REFLECTION
True love flows freely, without demands or conditions. When we release our "shoulds" about how others must behave, we create space for authentic relationships to flourish. Like a garden that thrives with gentle

tending rather than forced growth, relationships blossom when we let go of control. Today, practice loving others without demanding they follow your unspoken rules.

PRAYER
God of Love, teach me to love without conditions. When I'm tempted to demand specific behaviors, help me choose acceptance instead. Thank You for Your unconditional love. Lead me to reflect that love to others. Amen.

POSITIVE THOUGHT OF THE DAY
I choose to love without demands.

November 19th

Peace Through Release

SCRIPTURE
"Cast your burden on the Lord, and he will sustain you." - Psalm 55:22

REFLECTION
Peace grows when we release our grip on controlling others. Like setting down heavy stones we were never meant to carry, letting go of our mental "manuals" for others frees us to experience God's peace. When we trust Him with our relationships rather than trying to manage everyone's behavior, we find rest for our souls. Today, practice releasing your expectations to God's care.

PRAYER
Prince of Peace, help me find freedom in letting go. When I try to control others, remind me to trust Your care. Thank You for carrying my burdens. Guide me toward Your perfect peace. Amen.

POSITIVE THOUGHT OF THE DAY
I find peace in releasing control to God.

November 20th

Grace for Growth

SCRIPTURE
"Let us then approach God's throne of grace with confidence, so that we may receive mercy and find grace to help us in our time of need." - Hebrews 4:16

REFLECTION
God offers grace as we learn to release our expectations. When we stumble back into trying to control others, His mercy guides us toward freedom

again. Like children learning to walk, we grow stronger through each attempt to live in acceptance rather than control. Today, receive grace for your journey of learning to release expectations and trust God's work in others' lives.

PRAYER
God of Grace, strengthen me as I learn to release control. When I fall back into old patterns, help me begin again with hope. Thank You for Your patient guidance. Lead me in growing more like You. Amen.

POSITIVE THOUGHT OF THE DAY
I grow in grace as I release expectations.

November 21st

True Service vs. Fear

SCRIPTURE
"For you were called for freedom, brothers. But do not use this freedom as an opportunity for the flesh; rather, serve one another through love." - Galatians 5:13

REFLECTION
Genuine service flows from love, not fear of others' opinions. When we serve from authenticity rather than anxiety about pleasing others, we honor both God and our true selves. Like Jesus who served from love while maintaining clear boundaries, we're called to give from fullness rather than fear. Today, examine your motivations for service—do they spring from love or from fear of disapproval?

PRAYER
Lord of Love, help me serve from authentic care rather than fear. When I'm tempted to please others from anxiety, guide me toward genuine love. Thank You for modeling perfect service. Lead me to give from freedom rather than obligation. Amen.

POSITIVE THOUGHT OF THE DAY
I choose to serve from love, not fear.

November 22nd

Holy Boundaries

SCRIPTURE
"Let your 'Yes' mean 'Yes,' and your 'No' mean 'No.' Anything more is from the evil one." - Matthew 5:37

REFLECTION
Setting boundaries reflects God's truth in our lives. When we say 'yes' while our hearts whisper 'no,' we disconnect from authentic living. Like Christ who sometimes withdrew from crowds despite their demands, we need courage to align our words with our truth. Today, practice honest responses that honor both your limits and God's design for genuine relationship.

PRAYER
Divine Teacher, help me speak truth with love. When people-pleasing tempts me, strengthen me to be honest. Thank You for modeling healthy boundaries. Guide me in authentic living. Amen.

POSITIVE THOUGHT OF THE DAY
I honor God through truthful boundaries.

November 23rd

Finding Your True Yes

SCRIPTURE
"Each must do as already determined, without sadness or compulsion, for God loves a cheerful giver." - 2 Corinthians 9:7

REFLECTION
Joy flows from authentic service rather than obligated giving. When we serve from genuine desire rather than fear of disappointing others, we reflect God's cheerful giving. Like a stream flowing naturally rather than forced through artificial channels, our best service comes from heartfelt choice. Today, notice which commitments bring genuine joy versus strain.

PRAYER
Generous God, help me discern my true 'yes' from false obligation. When others' expectations pressure me, guide me toward authentic choices. Thank You for modeling cheerful giving. Lead me to serve with genuine joy. Amen.

POSITIVE THOUGHT OF THE DAY
I choose service that brings authentic joy.

November 24th

Worth Beyond Approval

SCRIPTURE
"You are precious in my eyes and honored, and I love you." - Isaiah 43:4

REFLECTION
Our worth rests in God's love, not others' approval. When we seek validation through constant people-pleasing, we miss the deep truth of our inherent value as God's beloved. Like a masterpiece already complete, we don't need others' praise to prove our worth. Today, remember that your value comes from being God's creation, not from pleasing others.

PRAYER
Loving Father, help me find my worth in Your unchanging love. When I seek approval through people-pleasing, remind me of my value in You. Thank You for cherishing me completely. Guide me to live from secure identity in You. Amen.

POSITIVE THOUGHT OF THE DAY
I rest secure in God's love, not others' approval.

November 25th

From Hurt to Healing

SCRIPTURE
"Bear with one another and, if anyone has a complaint against another, forgive each other; just as the Lord has forgiven you, so you also must forgive." - Colossians 3:13

REFLECTION
Forgiveness begins with acknowledging our hurt before God. Like bringing a wounded limb into healing light, we must first recognize our pain before transformation can begin. When we resist forgiveness, we carry unnecessary burdens that weigh down our spirits. Today, practice bringing your hurts to God, trusting that He can transform them into opportunities for grace.

PRAYER
Merciful Father, help me acknowledge my hurts before You. When unforgiveness weighs me down, guide me toward Your healing grace. Thank You for Your constant forgiveness. Lead me in releasing my burdens to You. Amen.

POSITIVE THOUGHT OF THE DAY
I bring my hurts to God for healing.

November 26th
Daily Steps of Grace

SCRIPTURE
"Then Peter approaching asked him, 'Lord, if my brother sins against me, how often must I forgive him? As many as seven times?' Jesus answered, 'I say to you, not seven times but seventy-seven times.'" - Matthew 18:21-22

REFLECTION
Forgiveness often requires repeated choices to release hurt. Like exercising a muscle, each choice to forgive strengthens our capacity for grace. When old hurts resurface, we can choose again to forgive, knowing that each decision moves us closer to freedom. Today, practice choosing forgiveness not once but as often as needed.

PRAYER
Patient Lord, strengthen me in choosing forgiveness repeatedly. When old hurts resurface, help me choose grace again. Thank You for Your endless mercy. Guide me in making forgiveness a daily practice. Amen.

POSITIVE THOUGHT OF THE DAY
I choose forgiveness as often as needed.

November 27th
Forgiveness Frees Us

SCRIPTURE
"Be kind to one another, tenderhearted, forgiving one another, as God in Christ has forgiven you." - Ephesians 4:32

REFLECTION
Unforgiveness binds us more than those who hurt us. When we hold onto grudges, we carry burdens that God never intended us to bear. Like setting down heavy stones that slow our journey, releasing unforgiveness frees us to move forward in grace. Today, notice where unforgiveness weighs you down and choose to release its burden.

PRAYER
God of Freedom, help me release the weight of unforgiveness. When I'm tempted to hold grudges, remind me that forgiveness frees me. Thank You for showing me a better way. Lead me toward the lightness of letting go. Amen.

POSITIVE THOUGHT OF THE DAY
I find freedom through forgiveness.

November 28th

Growing Through Grace

SCRIPTURE
"Get rid of all bitterness, rage and anger, brawling and slander, along with every form of malice. Be kind and compassionate to one another, forgiving each other, just as in Christ God forgave you." - Ephesians 4:31-32

REFLECTION
Each act of forgiveness transforms us more into Christ's image. When we extend mercy to others—and ourselves—we participate in God's work of grace. Like seeds that grow through consistent nurture, our capacity for forgiveness expands with practice. Today, consider how forgiveness might help you grow spiritually stronger.

PRAYER
Divine Teacher, help me grow through practicing forgiveness. When bitterness tempts me, guide me toward grace. Thank You for Your transforming love. Lead me in becoming more like You through forgiveness. Amen.

POSITIVE THOUGHT OF THE DAY
I grow stronger through choosing forgiveness.

November 29th

Small Steps of Stewardship

SCRIPTURE
"Do you not know that your body is a temple of the holy Spirit within you?" - 1 Corinthians 6:19

REFLECTION
Caring for our health becomes holy work when approached with gentle wisdom. Rather than attempting dramatic transformations, God often invites us to grow through small, faithful steps. Like morning dew that gradually nourishes soil, small healthy choices compound into significant change. Today, consider what single small step you might take to better care for your body-temple.

PRAYER
Divine Healer, help me care for this temple with gentle wisdom. When I'm tempted toward harsh changes, guide me to sustainable steps. Thank You for this body You've given me. Lead me in faithful stewardship. Amen.

November 30th

Grace for Growth

SCRIPTURE
"For God did not give us a spirit of fear but rather of power and love and self-control." - 2 Timothy 1:7

REFLECTION
Health changes flow best from love rather than fear. When we approach wellness from God's perspective of gentle power rather than harsh judgment, sustainable transformation becomes possible. Like plants that thrive with patient tending, our health flourishes through grace-filled attention. Today, practice replacing fearful thoughts about health with loving choices.

PRAYER
Loving Father, help me approach health changes with grace. When fear tempts me toward harshness, guide me to gentle strength. Thank You for Your patient love. Lead me in making choices from power rather than fear. Amen.

POSITIVE THOUGHT OF THE DAY
I choose health with love, not fear.

December

December 1st

Community's Strength

SCRIPTURE
"Two are better than one, because they have a good return for their labor."
- Ecclesiastes 4:9

REFLECTION
God designed us to grow stronger through community. When we attempt health changes alone, we miss His provision of support through others. Like stones that form a stronger wall together than apart, we achieve more when united in our wellness journey. Today, consider how sharing your health goals might invite divine support through others.

PRAYER
Lord of Community, help me accept support in my health journey. When pride tempts me to go alone, remind me of Your design for connection. Thank You for providing helpers. Guide me to receive support with grace. Amen.

POSITIVE THOUGHT OF THE DAY
I grow stronger through shared support.

December 2nd

Wisdom in Waiting

SCRIPTURE
"But those who hope in the Lord will renew their strength." - Isaiah 40:31

REFLECTION
True health transformation requires holy patience. Like seeds that grow through seasons rather than overnight, lasting change develops through consistent small choices. When we trust God's timing rather than demanding instant results, we align with His pattern of growth. Today, practice finding peace in gradual progress toward wellness.

PRAYER
Patient God, help me trust Your timing in my health journey. When I desire instant change, remind me of Your perfect pace. Thank You for guiding my growth. Lead me in making steady progress. Amen.

POSITIVE THOUGHT OF THE DAY
I trust God's timing in my health journey.

December 3rd

Planning for Peace

SCRIPTURE
"Peace I leave with you; my peace I give to you. Not as the world gives do I give it to you. Do not let your hearts be troubled or afraid." - John 14:27

REFLECTION
Like Mary preparing for Jesus' birth in less-than-ideal circumstances, we too can find peace amid holiday challenges. When we prioritize our spiritual wellbeing before tackling celebrations, we create space for God's peace to flourish. Setting aside even brief moments for prayer and reflection helps ground us in what truly matters.

PRAYER
Lord, help me prioritize peace in this busy season. When holiday pressures mount, remind me to pause and connect with You. Thank You for offering perfect peace. Guide me in making choices that protect my inner calm. Amen.

POSITIVE THOUGHT OF THE DAY
I choose peace before productivity.

December 4th

Grace in Family Gatherings

SCRIPTURE
"Put on then, as God's chosen ones, holy and beloved, heartfelt compassion, kindness, humility, gentleness, and patience." - Colossians 3:12

REFLECTION
Family gatherings often test our peace, but they also offer opportunities to practice Christ's love. When challenging dynamics arise, we can respond with prepared grace rather than reactive tension. Like Jesus who remained peaceful amid difficult situations, we too can maintain inner calm through thoughtful responses.

PRAYER
Gentle Father, help me respond to family dynamics with grace. When tensions rise, guide me toward peaceful responses. Thank You for the gift of family. Lead me in showing Your love through my actions. Amen.

POSITIVE THOUGHT OF THE DAY
I choose graceful responses in family situations.

December 5th
Simplifying with Purpose

SCRIPTURE
"Martha, Martha, you are anxious and worried about many things. There is need of only one thing." - Luke 10:41-42

REFLECTION
True holiday joy often emerges from simplicity rather than complexity. When we release the pressure to create perfect celebrations, we make room for meaningful moments. Like Mary choosing "the better part" at Jesus' feet, we can select what truly matters and let go of unnecessary obligations.

PRAYER
Lord of Simplicity, help me choose what truly matters. When I feel pressured to do everything, remind me of what's essential. Thank You for showing me a better way. Guide me in creating meaningful celebrations. Amen.

POSITIVE THOUGHT OF THE DAY
I find joy in choosing what matters most.

December 6th
Choosing Daily Joy

SCRIPTURE
"Rejoice in the Lord always. I shall say it again: rejoice!" - Philippians 4:4

REFLECTION
Joy becomes a powerful choice in the midst of holiday imperfection. When we intentionally look for moments of delight - a child's laughter, quiet morning prayer, shared family traditions - we participate in God's gift of joy. Like the shepherds who found joy in a humble manger, we can discover beauty in simple moments.

PRAYER
God of Joy, help me notice and celebrate small blessings. When perfectionism tempts me, guide me toward genuine delight. Thank You for daily gifts of joy. Lead me in choosing happiness amid the holiday season. Amen.

POSITIVE THOUGHT OF THE DAY
I actively choose joy each day.

December 7th

Finding Daily Wonder

SCRIPTURE
"Open my eyes, that I may see wonderful things." - Psalm 119:18

REFLECTION
Wonder isn't limited to special seasons - it's available in every ordinary moment. When we approach life with open hearts, even simple experiences become sacred opportunities. Like children discovering the world anew each day, we can choose to see God's hand in unexpected places. Today, look for moments of surprise and beauty in your routine.

PRAYER
Lord of Wonder, help me see Your presence in everyday moments. When life feels ordinary, open my eyes to Your extraordinary gifts. Thank You for countless daily miracles. Guide me in discovering beauty in the familiar. Amen.

POSITIVE THOUGHT OF THE DAY
I choose to find wonder in ordinary moments.

December 8th

Gratitude's Gift

SCRIPTURE
"Give thanks to the Lord, for he is good, his mercy endures forever." - Psalm 107:1

REFLECTION
Gratitude transforms ordinary days into extraordinary experiences. When we pause to notice our blessings, we participate in divine joy. Like Mary treasuring moments in her heart, we can collect daily gifts of grace - a child's laugh, morning sunlight, shared meals. Today, practice seeing your life through the lens of thankfulness.

PRAYER
Generous God, help me cultivate a grateful heart. When I take blessings for granted, remind me to pause in thanks. Thank You for countless daily gifts. Guide me in maintaining an attitude of gratitude. Amen.

POSITIVE THOUGHT OF THE DAY
I transform ordinary moments through gratitude.

December 9th

Spirit of Giving

SCRIPTURE
"It is more blessed to give than to receive." - Acts 20:35

REFLECTION
The joy of giving isn't confined to special occasions. Each day offers opportunities to share God's love through simple acts of kindness. When we extend ourselves in service, we participate in divine generosity. Like Christ who gave freely, we can find daily ways to brighten others' lives through small gestures of care.

PRAYER
Loving Father, help me embrace opportunities to give. When focused on myself, remind me to look outward with love. Thank You for the joy of serving others. Guide me in sharing Your love daily. Amen.

POSITIVE THOUGHT OF THE DAY
I find joy in daily acts of giving.

December 10th

Faith's Daily Light

SCRIPTURE
"Your word is a lamp for my feet, a light for my path." - Psalm 119:105

REFLECTION
Faith brings light to every ordinary day. When we stay connected to God through prayer and scripture, routine moments become sacred encounters. Like a familiar path illuminated by dawn's light, daily spiritual practices reveal beauty in the familiar. Today, let your faith transform ordinary moments into holy experiences.

PRAYER
Divine Light, help me see Your presence in each day. When routine dulls my spirit, awaken me to Your grace. Thank You for illuminating my path. Guide me in maintaining wonder through faith. Amen.

POSITIVE THOUGHT OF THE DAY
I find sacred moments through daily faith.

December 11th
Choosing Holiday Peace

SCRIPTURE
"I have told you these things, so that in me you may have peace. In this world you will have trouble. But take heart! I have overcome the world."
- John 16:33

REFLECTION
Holiday stress often comes from trying to do everything perfectly. When we release unrealistic expectations and focus on what truly matters, peace naturally follows. Like Mary choosing "the better part," we can select activities that align with our values and bring genuine joy. Today, consider what you might need to release to make room for peace.

PRAYER
Prince of Peace, help me choose activities that bring true joy. When overwhelmed by holiday pressures, guide me toward what matters most. Thank You for showing me a simpler path. Lead me in creating peaceful celebrations. Amen.

POSITIVE THOUGHT OF THE DAY
I choose peace over perfection this season.

December 12th
Future Peace Today

SCRIPTURE
"Therefore do not worry about tomorrow, for tomorrow will worry about itself." - Matthew 6:34

REFLECTION
Planning with intention helps create the peaceful future we desire. When we envision our ideal holiday experience and work backward, we discover what truly deserves our time and energy today. Like a gardener preparing soil before planting, thoughtful preparation now yields peace later. Consider what small steps today will create the peaceful holiday you desire.

PRAYER
Divine Guide, help me plan wisely for peaceful celebrations. When anxiety about the future arises, bring me back to present peace. Thank You for guiding my steps. Lead me in creating meaningful moments. Amen.

POSITIVE THOUGHT OF THE DAY
I create future peace through present choices.

December 13th

Truth in Love

SCRIPTURE
"Therefore each of you must put off falsehood and speak truthfully to your neighbor." - Ephesians 4:25

REFLECTION
Speaking our truth with love creates space for authentic joy. When we honestly express our needs and boundaries, we honor both ourselves and others. Like Christ who spoke with gentle clarity, we can communicate our limits while maintaining connection. Today, practice speaking your truth with kindness about holiday commitments.

PRAYER
Lord of Truth, help me communicate honestly with love. When tempted to please others at my expense, grant me courage for truth-telling. Thank You for modeling authentic love. Guide me in setting loving boundaries. Amen.

POSITIVE THOUGHT OF THE DAY
I speak my truth with gentle love.

December 14th

Abundance in Christ

SCRIPTURE
"And my God will meet all your needs according to the riches of his glory in Christ Jesus." - Philippians 4:19

REFLECTION
True abundance flows from recognizing God's provision in every moment. When we shift from scarcity to gratitude, we discover we already have enough - enough time, resources, and love to share. Like Jesus multiplying loaves and fishes, God provides exactly what we need. Today, notice where abundance already exists in your life.

PRAYER
Generous Provider, help me see Your abundance all around. When scarcity thoughts arise, remind me of Your faithful provision. Thank You for meeting all my needs. Guide me to share from Your plenty. Amen.

POSITIVE THOUGHT OF THE DAY
I live in God's abundant provision.

December 15th
Daily Assessment of Joy

SCRIPTURE
"Test everything; retain what is good." - 1 Thessalonians 5:21

REFLECTION
Like taking inventory of a garden's growth, regular spiritual assessment helps us cultivate joy. When we pause to measure our happiness, health, and holiness, we discover areas ready for divine nurturing. Today, consider where you stand in these areas, not to judge, but to invite God's transforming grace into specific aspects of your life.

PRAYER
Divine Gardener, help me assess my spiritual growth with honesty. When I notice areas needing attention, guide me toward positive change. Thank You for Your patient cultivation. Lead me in growing closer to Your vision for my life. Amen.

POSITIVE THOUGHT OF THE DAY
I grow through mindful spiritual assessment.

December 16th

Present Grace

SCRIPTURE
"Behold, now is a very acceptable time; behold, now is the day of salvation."
- 2 Corinthians 6:2

REFLECTION
Our current thoughts shape our future more than past experiences. When we focus on present choices rather than previous shortcomings, we open ourselves to God's transforming power. Like seeds that sprout only in current conditions, our growth depends on today's spiritual nurturing. Practice being fully present to God's work in your life today.

PRAYER
Lord of Now, help me focus on present opportunities for growth. When past regrets surface, draw me back to Your current grace. Thank You for fresh beginnings each day. Guide me in making choices that reflect Your love. Amen.

POSITIVE THOUGHT OF THE DAY
I choose growth in this present moment.

December 17th

Steps Toward Holiness

SCRIPTURE
"One thing I do: forgetting what lies behind and straining forward to what lies ahead, I press on toward the goal." - Philippians 3:13-14

REFLECTION
Progress in faith comes through small, consistent choices. When we regularly assess our spiritual journey, we discover opportunities for deeper connection with God. Like climbing a mountain one step at a time, holiness develops through daily dedication. Today, notice where you can take one small step toward deeper faith.

PRAYER
Patient Teacher, help me recognize opportunities for spiritual growth. When I feel stuck, show me the next small step. Thank You for guiding my journey. Lead me closer to You one choice at a time. Amen.

POSITIVE THOUGHT OF THE DAY
I grow in holiness through daily choices.

December 18th

Balanced Growth

SCRIPTURE
"May the God of peace make you perfectly holy and may you be preserved whole and complete." - 1 Thessalonians 5:23

REFLECTION
True wellbeing embraces spiritual, emotional, and physical health. When we tend to each aspect of our lives with intentional care, we honor God's design for wholeness. Like a tree growing strong through balanced nurture of roots, trunk, and branches, we thrive when caring for every dimension of our being.

PRAYER
God of Wholeness, help me nurture every aspect of my life. When I neglect any area of growth, restore my balance. Thank You for designing me with such care. Guide me in tending to my complete wellbeing. Amen.

POSITIVE THOUGHT OF THE DAY
I grow in balanced wholeness with God's help.

December 19th

Peace in Progress

SCRIPTURE
"May the God of hope fill you with all joy and peace in believing." - Romans 15:13

REFLECTION
Small steps lead to meaningful growth in faith and life. When we focus on gradual progress rather than dramatic change, we create sustainable transformation. Like building physical strength through consistent exercise, spiritual and emotional growth develops through steady practice. Today, choose one small step toward your spiritual goals.

PRAYER
Patient God, help me trust the power of small changes. When I rush toward perfection, remind me that steady progress matters. Thank You for guiding my growth. Lead me in taking faithful steps forward. Amen.

POSITIVE THOUGHT OF THE DAY
I grow stronger through small, faithful steps.

December 20th

Sacred Moments

SCRIPTURE
"Be still and know that I am God." - Psalm 46:11

REFLECTION
Holiness blooms in everyday moments when we pause to notice God's presence. Whether in nature's beauty, quiet prayer, or acts of service, sacred encounters await our attention. Like collecting precious stones, we gather these holy moments into a treasury of faith. Today, look for divine fingerprints in ordinary experiences.

PRAYER
Lord of Wonder, open my eyes to Your presence in daily life. When I rush past sacred moments, help me pause and notice. Thank You for countless holy encounters. Guide me in recognizing Your presence. Amen.

POSITIVE THOUGHT OF THE DAY
I find sacred moments in everyday life.

December 21st

Joy's True Source

SCRIPTURE
"You will show me the path to life, abounding joy in your presence." -
Psalm 16:11

REFLECTION
True joy flows from accepting life's full range of emotions while staying anchored in God's love. Rather than seeking constant happiness, we find peace in knowing that every feeling serves a purpose in our spiritual journey. Like a tree that bends with changing winds, we grow stronger through embracing all seasons of the soul.

PRAYER
Divine Teacher, help me find peace in life's emotional seasons. When I resist difficult feelings, remind me of Your constant presence. Thank You for joy's deeper meaning. Guide me toward authentic living. Amen.

POSITIVE THOUGHT OF THE DAY
I find true joy in God's faithful presence.

December 22nd

Wholeness in Growth

SCRIPTURE
"May your whole spirit and soul and body be preserved blameless for the coming of our Lord Jesus Christ." - 1 Thessalonians 5:23

REFLECTION
God invites us to grow in body, mind, and spirit. When we tend to our whole being—physical, emotional, and spiritual health—we honor His design for our lives. Like a garden that needs various forms of care to flourish, our wellbeing requires balanced attention. Today, consider how you might nurture each aspect of your life.

PRAYER
Creator God, help me care for my whole being. When I neglect any area of growth, restore my balance. Thank You for designing me with such care. Guide me in honoring Your plan for my wellbeing. Amen.

POSITIVE THOUGHT OF THE DAY
I grow in wholeness through balanced care.

December 23rd

Choosing Love Daily

SCRIPTURE
"And now these three remain: faith, hope, and love, but the greatest of these is love." - 1 Corinthians 13:13

REFLECTION
Love isn't just a response to others' actions—it's a choice we make independently. When we shift from expecting others to earn our love to choosing love regardless of circumstances, we reflect God's unconditional heart. Today, notice where you've placed conditions on love and consider choosing love simply because it enriches your own spirit.

PRAYER
Lord of Love, help me choose love regardless of circumstances. When I'm tempted to withhold love, remind me of Your unconditional grace. Thank You for teaching me true love. Guide me in loving freely. Amen.

POSITIVE THOUGHT OF THE DAY
I choose love without conditions.

December 24th

Freedom in Loving

SCRIPTURE
"We love because he first loved us." - 1 John 4:19

REFLECTION
True freedom comes when we release others from meeting our expectations before receiving our love. Like God who loves us despite our imperfections, we can choose to love others without requiring them to change. Today, practice loving freely, recognizing that your capacity to love isn't dependent on others' behavior but on your own choice.

PRAYER
Divine Love, help me love others without conditions. When I create rules for giving love, guide me toward genuine acceptance. Thank You for loving me freely. Lead me in extending that same grace to others. Amen.

POSITIVE THOUGHT OF THE DAY
I find freedom in loving unconditionally.

December 25th

Love's Inner Source

SCRIPTURE
"Love is patient, love is kind... it keeps no record of wrongs." - 1 Corinthians 13:4-5

REFLECTION
Love's power flows from within, not from external circumstances. When we understand that our ability to love comes from our own thoughts and choices, we discover an endless wellspring of compassion. Like a deep river that flows regardless of surface conditions, our love can remain constant despite others' actions.

PRAYER
Merciful Father, help me find love's source within. When external circumstances challenge my love, strengthen my inner resolve. Thank You for this limitless capacity to love. Guide me in maintaining steady compassion. Amen.

POSITIVE THOUGHT OF THE DAY
I access love's endless inner source.

December 26th

Growing in Love

SCRIPTURE
"Above all, love each other deeply, because love covers over a multitude of sins." - 1 Peter 4:8

REFLECTION
Each choice to love expands our capacity for compassion. When we consciously choose love, especially in challenging moments, we grow spiritually stronger. Like muscles that develop through exercise, our ability to love unconditionally strengthens through practice. Today, view difficult relationships as opportunities to strengthen your loving heart.

PRAYER
God of Growth, help me strengthen my capacity to love. When relationships challenge me, remind me that these are opportunities for growth. Thank You for teaching me deeper love. Lead me in expanding my heart's boundaries. Amen.

POSITIVE THOUGHT OF THE DAY
I grow stronger through choosing love.

December 27th

Light in Darkness

SCRIPTURE
"The light shines in the darkness, and the darkness has not overcome it."
- John 1:5

REFLECTION
Even in our darkest moments, a small sliver of light remains visible when we choose to seek it. Like prisoners finding hope in the faintest ray of sunshine, we can focus on small blessings until they illuminate our path. Prayer, scripture, service to others - these become beacons leading us from darkness to light. Today, search for one point of light in any challenging situation.

PRAYER
Lord of Light, help me find Your presence in dark times. When shadows overwhelm, guide my eyes toward Your light. Thank You for never leaving me in darkness. Lead me toward Your eternal brightness. Amen.

POSITIVE THOUGHT OF THE DAY
I choose to focus on light rather than darkness.

December 28th

Growing in Light

SCRIPTURE
"Your word is a lamp for my feet, a light for my path." - Psalm 119:105

REFLECTION
Growth comes through deliberately turning toward light instead of dwelling in shadows. When we focus on prayer, positive action, and authentic relationships, these small lights expand to illuminate our whole path. Like a sunrise that begins with one bright ray, spiritual growth starts with choosing one life-giving thought or action. Today, nurture what brings light to your life.

PRAYER
Divine Light, help me cultivate what brings Your brightness. When tempted toward darkness, remind me to choose Your way. Thank You for showing me paths of light. Guide me in growing toward Your radiance. Amen.

POSITIVE THOUGHT OF THE DAY
I grow stronger by choosing light each day.

December 29th

New Beliefs, New Life

SCRIPTURE
"Do not conform to the pattern of this world, but be transformed by the renewing of your mind." - Romans 12:2

REFLECTION
Growth begins with believing new truths about ourselves. When we release old thought patterns that no longer serve us, we create space for divine transformation. Like a garden being replanted, our minds need regular tending to nurture new beliefs. Today, identify one limiting belief you're ready to replace with truth.

PRAYER
Divine Teacher, help me release old beliefs that limit my growth. When doubt surfaces, strengthen my new faith in what's possible. Thank You for transforming my mind. Guide me in believing Your truth about my life. Amen.

POSITIVE THOUGHT OF THE DAY
I cultivate new beliefs that align with God's truth.

December 30th

Building Faith Step by Step

SCRIPTURE
"For we walk by faith, not by sight." - 2 Corinthians 5:7

REFLECTION
Faith grows through small, consistent choices to believe. When we feel resistance to new beliefs, we can take gradual steps rather than expecting instant transformation. Like climbing a ladder one rung at a time, we build stronger faith through steady practice. Today, take one small step toward believing God's bigger vision for your life.

PRAYER
Patient Father, strengthen my faith one step at a time. When changes feel overwhelming, remind me that growth comes gradually. Thank You for guiding each step. Lead me in building stronger beliefs. Amen.

POSITIVE THOUGHT OF THE DAY
I grow in faith one choice at a time.

December 31st

Future Faith

SCRIPTURE
"Forgetting what lies behind and straining forward to what lies ahead, I press on toward the goal." - Philippians 3:13-14

REFLECTION
Our future isn't limited by our past - it's shaped by what we choose to believe today. When we focus on God's possibilities rather than previous limitations, we open ourselves to transformation. Like runners fixing their eyes on the finish line, we can focus on what we're becoming rather than what we've been.

PRAYER
God of New Beginnings, help me believe in the future You see for me. When past limitations surface, draw my focus to Your possibilities. Thank You for endless fresh starts. Guide me toward Your vision. Amen.

POSITIVE THOUGHT OF THE DAY
I choose to believe in God's vision for my future.

About the Author

Danielle Thienel is a certified life coach and Catholic mother with a passion for helping overwhelmed moms find peace, balance, and joy in their daily lives. Based in Nashville, Tennessee, she combines impactful life coaching tools with Catholic spirituality to guide women toward more purposeful and peaceful living.

As host of The Peaceful Mind Podcast for Catholic Moms (with over 250 episodes), Danielle reaches thousands of mothers seeking practical wisdom for their faith journey. Her coaching practice, certified through The Life Coach School, has helped countless women transform their approach to motherhood over the past five years.

Danielle draws from her experience as a wife of nearly 25 years and mother of three to relate authentically to women's daily challenges. Her own morning devotional practice, inspired by works like Sarah Young's Jesus Calling, led her to create this devotional that weaves together Catholic faith, practical wisdom, and life coaching principles.

She is also the author of The Cyclone Mom Method, The Peaceful Mind Bible for Busy Moms, and The Divine Time Solution, all focused on empowering Catholic mothers to embrace their God-given abilities and find more peace in their vocation.

To learn more about Danielle and her offerings, visit daniellethienel.com. Contact her directly at danielle@daniellethienel.com.

www.ingramcontent.com/pod-product-compliance
Lightning Source LLC
Chambersburg PA
CBHW051524150726
47997CB00001B/373